Challenges in Pastoral Care: Divorce and Remarriage

Charles Joanides, PhD, LMFT

Department of Marriage and Family
Greek Orthodox Archdiocese of America
New York, New York

© 2013 Greek Orthodox Archdiocese of America

Published by the Department of Marriage and Family
Greek Orthodox Archdiocese of America
79 Saint Basil Rd.
Garrison, NY 10524

ISBN 978-1-58438-038-2 (waiting for number)

The icon on the cover of Christ the Good Shepherd is used with
permission from Athanasios Clark www.tomclarkicons.com.

To all the spouses and couples
who've taught me so much
about the debilitating effects of divorce
and the resilience of the human spirit.
May our Lord richly bless you.

TABLE OF CONTENTS

A Note to Clergy

This year, approximately two million couples will get married in our country and one million marriages will end in divorce. We live in a culture of divorce, and as you well know, Greek Orthodox Christians are not isolated from this reality. Challenges in Pastoral Care: Divorce and Remarriage is an initial effort to address this dire pastoral issue. With God's help, our hope is to continue developing resources to aid clergy and lay workers as they minister to the faithful.

As you will note, the articles in this resource focus upon themes of marriage and divorce. While many may choose to read the entire resource, the articles were written to be used strategically. The following suggestions are some ways to help you navigate your use of this resource.

1. All articles can be used for educational purposes.

2. The first three articles can be used in premarital and marital counseling.

3. The first three articles can be shared with spouses and conflicted couples. They offer a number of compelling reasons why couples should struggle to recapture marital satisfaction and oneness.

4. Articles four through nine address marital conflict and divorce. They can be shared when spouses and couples who are struggling with finances, infidelity, domestic violence and sexual addictions.

5. The article entitled "Recovering from Divorce" addresses issues divorced persons encounter in their efforts to find personal, family and spiritual stability and well-being after divorce.

6. The final article entitled "Remarriage and Step-Family Challenges" can be shared with couples where one or both partners are entering a second marriage. This article outlines many of the key challenges that couples encounter when they remarry and form step families.

It is my hope that the contents of this resource will prove helpful to you in your efforts to address the thorny pastoral issues of marital conflict, divorce and remarriage—to God's glory and the salvation of those whom you will seek to counsel.

FOREWORD

Challenges in Pastoral Care: Divorce and Remarriage by Rev. Dr. Charles Joanides is a welcomed resource and the first of its kind, engaging the theme of divorce and remarriage from a pastoral, psychological, and practical Orthodox Christian perspective. Written primarily as a handbook for Greek Orthodox Christians, this volume nevertheless may easily become a "primer" on divorce and remarriage for many Orthodox Christians today.

Through this well-written book, Fr. Charles offers credible and concise pastoral care and advice. Well-researched, yet easy to read, readers may feel as if Fr. Charles is speaking with them personally in his office or visiting with them in their home. Anchored deeply in the theological vision of Christian marriage as understood by the Orthodox Church, this gently persuasive pastoral writing style is important, as it helps convey much information that has been distilled through his rich experience as a Greek Orthodox pastor and licensed marriage and family therapist.

We humans sometimes become psychologically overwhelmed and flooded during times of marital and family crisis. This may cause us to abruptly react in an unhelpful manner rather than thoughtfully responding to the challenges at hand. Fr. Charles knows this very well. And when persons sometimes find themselves in the throes of a crisis, relating pertinent and credible information as well as advice on moving forward tends to be significantly more difficult to undertake. Here Fr. Charles is arguably at his best, as he discerns and offers necessary and even vital information both clearly and respectfully. He also offers to the reader in a gentle and persuasive manner various spiritually (and psychologically) healthy options to consider, options that may help give real hope for better days to come.

This multitasking is actually an important strength of the book, as the author identifies and succinctly discusses a number of serious challenges that touch the majority of marriages in contemporary society, such as: why marriages fail, the myths about divorce, strategies to help rethink—and thus avoid—divorce, money and divorce, infidelity, domestic violence, sexual addictions, recovering from divorce, and remarriage/stepfamily challenges. By reviewing these various challenging pastoral topics, Fr. Charles also directly relates the Church's vision of marriage to these specific concerns with clarity, as well as charity.

Clearly, this very helpful book in no way strives to replace necessary and appropriate spiritual direction or pastoral counseling within the parish or professional consultations with qualified licensed mental health professionals. Nevertheless, it is partly through the process of respecting these limitations that *Challenges in Pastoral Care: Divorce and Remarriage* may prove to become a succinct, contemporary "primer" on the application of the vision of Orthodox Christian marriage while "under fire," so to speak. Furthermore, this volume also offers simple to understand "take-away" concepts and suggested resources to assist with setting a better course forward. For this reason, in addition to this handbook being an essential resource and pastoral aid for clergy who wish to offer parishioners an "Orthodox first response" resource for their marital health, many sections of this book may be adapted as timely study modules for adult education programs, marital enrichment curricula, and/or small discussion groups of older teens and adults of all ages.

May this long-awaited resource be a blessing to all those who read it, and may it serve as a vehicle of encouragement, pertinent introductory information, trustworthy guidance, and hope for persons seeking help with their community or communion (koinonia) of marriage, so that together, through the blessing of the all-merciful Lord, we may more fully "hear the word of God and do it" (Luke 11:28).

(Pres.) Dr. Kyriaki Karidoyanes FitzGerald, MDiv, PhD
Adjunct Professor in Theology, Holy Cross Greek Orthodox School of Theology
Licensed Psychologist, Mass. Health Service Provider
Pastoral Counselor, American Association of Pastoral Counselors
Marriage and Family Mediator, American Association of Mediators

October 6, 2012
The Feastday of St. Thomas the Apostle
Holy Cross Greek Orthodox School of Theology
Brookline, MA

INTRODUCTION

Why a Resource on Divorce and Remarriage?

You might be wondering why our Archdiocese has produced a resource devoted to divorce and remarriage issues. From the outset, it should be emphasized that the Archdiocese is not encouraging nor acquiescing to our society's high divorce and remarriage rates. The Archdiocese remains firmly devoted to the Church's theology of marriage, which professes that the marriage bond is eternal, and the Archdiocese finds these social trends lamentable. Despite its position regarding divorce and remarriage, it also acknowledges humankind's vulnerabilities and seeks to offer its faithful a second and even a third chance to remarry and struggle toward salvation.

So, if this resource is not somehow condoning high divorce rates, why has it been produced? The first reason is related to the following statistics: The divorce rate among couples marrying for the first time is between 45 and 50%; for couples marrying for a second time, it is between 60 and 67%, and for couples marrying a third time, it is between 70 and 73% (PressTV 2012). In addition, the divorce rate among unaffiliated Christians is around 50%, and, among Christians who attend services weekly, it presently stands at around 38%. And although reliable statistics are not available for Orthodox Christians, it can be unequivocally stated that we are not immune to these trends.

A second, equally important reason for the publication of this resource is related to results from a recent research study conducted by the Department of Marriage and Family entitled, *The Orthodox Family in America at Home and in the Church: A Study of Families in the Greek Orthodox Archdiocese of America* (2010). Results from this study indicate the need for psycho-educational materials that are decidedly Orthodox for married couples and families. To that end, this resource, along with many that will follow, is a response to requests from respondents to the study.

Third, because divorce and remarriage are serious issues that challenge our faithful, and because there is a deficit of resources addressing these challenges from a pastoral perspective, as a department we determined that these topics were appropriately suited to our objective of continuing to meet the complex marital and family challenges that our faithful encounter and need help with.

Content

The first chapter, entitled "Why Marriages Fail," describes a very slippery slope that many couples get caught on. This slope leads couples toward marital meltdown and divorce. The second chapter, "Myths about Divorce," addresses common myths relating to divorce that people absorb simply by living in a divorce culture (Defoe Whitehead 1996). The third chapter, entitled "Rethinking Divorce: Ten Strategies That Can Help," seeks to challenge spouses who are dissatisfied with their marriage and are thinking about this option as a solution to their marital problems. The fourth chapter, entitled "Money Matters: How Finances Impact Marriage and Divorce," addresses a couple's finances. It describes how differences related to money matters can undermine marriage. Suggestions are offered to help couples avoid many of the typical pitfalls that undermine marital satisfaction and contribute to divorce. The fifth and sixth chapters, entitled "Recovering from Infidelity, Parts I and II," provide information to spouses and couples seeking to recover from infidelity. These chapters maintain that although infidelity is a serious breach, couples can and do recover from this breach. The seventh chapter, entitled "Domestic Violence and Marriage," addresses the toxic effects of physical violence and seeks to provide helpful information to victims of domestic violence. The eighth chapter, entitled "No More Secrets: Sexual Addictions and Compulsions," describes how cybersexual activities undermine personal, couple, and family well-being. This chapter encourages those afflicted with this problem to find help. The ninth chapter, entitled "Recovering from Divorce," acknowledges that marriages end and seeks to map the territory of recovery that people follow in their efforts to recover from divorce. The final chapter, entitled "Remarriage and Stepfamily Challenges," acknowledges that people remarry and often form stepfamilies. These families encounter unique challenges in their efforts to cultivate oneness and blend two families into one.

Taken together, these chapters address many of the chief pastoral challenges related to divorce and remarriage that face our faithful. They are decidedly Christ-centered and written in a readable style that seeks to provide useful and needed information to our faithful. Those who desire additional copies can download them directly from either of the following websites: www.interfaith.org or www.family.goarch.org.

Using This Resource

As the title implies, this resource has been written for Orthodox Christians who are struggling with challenges and issues related to divorce and remarriage. Together with this target readership, other persons—especially those who have a Christian faith background—can also utilize this information.

Pastors who encounter questions and concerns related to divorce, infidelity, domestic violence, pornography, divorce recovery, and stepfamily challenges can also profit from this information. At a minimum, this resource can decidedly enhance their pastoral guidance and provide them with useful handouts that can be downloaded from the above websites or simply copied and shared. Additional copies are also readily available through the Department of Marriage and Family.

Not a Substitute for Professional Help

As useful as these articles may be, it should be noted that they are not a substitute for professional help. In addition to the help they receive from their pastor, spouses and couples who are struggling with any of the challenges discussed in this resource are strongly advised to seek professional help. Further, clergy who lack advanced training in these areas are also encouraged to find professionals in their area who have special training and experience working with the various individual disorders and marital challenges discussed in this resource. Together with the pastoral and spiritual guidance clergy can offer, collaboration with psychotherapists can prove invaluable to persons, couples, and families struggling with these clinical and pastoral challenges.

Acknowledgments

The Department of Marriage and Family would like to would like to thank Archbishop Demetrios of America for his steadfast support. His continued guidance and vision have been crucial to this new ministry's efforts to fulfill the needs of persons, couples, and families in our Archdiocese. Without His Eminence's vision and guidance, the work that has been produced and remains to be produced would not have been possible. As a department, we would also like to thank the members of Leadership 100 for their continued financial support, which has helped to make this resource a reality. We look forward to cultivating a long relationship with Leadership 100 as we continue to grow this vital ministry.

I am grateful to our director, Fr. Constantine L. Sitaras, for his capable leadership and tireless work to build the ministry for our families. I would also like to extend my gratitude to Kerry Pappas, MA, LMFT, for her many helpful suggestions and especially for her contributions to the chapter on domestic violence. Her many insightful additions strengthened this resource and made it better. Special thanks are also extended to Drs. Kyriaki Karidoyanes FitzGerald and Andrew Mercurio for their various useful recommendations. Finally, I would like to thank Melissa Tsongranis and Panayiotis Sakellariou for helping to facilitate the process that was required to make this resource a reality, to God's glory and our salvation. Amen.

Rev. Fr. Charles Joanides, PhD, LMFT
May 25, 2012

REFERENCES

- *The Divorce Culture: Rethinking Our Commitments to Marriage and Family.* Defoe Whitehead, B. 1996. New York: Vintage Books.

- *The Orthodox Family in America at Home and in the Church: A Study of Families in the Greek Orthodox Archdiocese of America.* Crea, T., and Krindatch, A. 2010. New York: Greek Orthodox Archdiocese of America.

- *PressTV.* 2011. "Quick Facts: America and divorce." Last modified March 17. http://www.presstv.ir/usdetail/170458.html.

WHY MARRIAGES FAIL

When we marry, we do not really understand what we are signing up for. We are in love and we want to be together. Some of us even believe that our union is a match made in heaven. On our wedding day, Christ joins us in marriage. We hear in the Epistle reading that we are called to love each other as Christ loves us. It is a wonderful day, filled with hopes and dreams. Numerous delicious expectations fill our hearts and minds. In the midst of those closest to us—our grandparents, parents, siblings, aunts, uncles, godparents, and closest friends—our wedding rings and crowns are blessed and exchanged, we drink together from the common cup, we dance Isaiah's dance around the table, we are blessed by our priest's homily, we share our first kiss as husband and wife, and we are rushed off to the reception. We receive endless prayerful best wishes. Cameras flash around us and capture many moments of joy for posterity. Indeed, on this blessed and seemingly perfect day, as Saint Paul's famous chapter on love states, our love is patient and kind; it is not arrogant or rude. Our love seems selfless and pure, and everything is good.

> COUPLES WHO BEGIN THEIR RELATIONSHIP AS SOUL MATES DRIFT APART AND SLOWLY FEEL MORE LIKE ROOMMATES, AND EVENTUALLY EVEN LIKE CELL MATES.

Then we return from the honeymoon, and life's unexpected circumstances and temptations begin to distract us. Soon our sins and shortcomings take hold of us, and Satan begins working overtime in our lives, until all that was worthy and good and beautiful seems like a lost dream. The oneness we heard about during our wedding preparations is forgotten, and many of us begin living self-centered and selfish existences. We enter into one combative exchange after another and into an endless number of differences, difficulties, and disagreements. The love we shared and promised one another is replaced with toxic feelings like anger, resentment, and bitterness. Soon we find ourselves on a very slippery slope that leads us to marital meltdown and divorce.

This chapter will describe, in harsh detail, why so many marriages are failing today—why perhaps your marriage is either failing or has failed. If you find the patterns and exchanges that follow all too familiar, you probably needed help yesterday, and I would urge you to get the help you need before you reach a point of no return. With lots of hard work, the love you once shared can still be recaptured. It is my hope that what follows will be a wake-up call for you to seek help for your marriage, because—with the grace of God, your efforts, and the help of a competent marriage therapist—you can reclaim your marriage.

A Very Predictable Path

According to Dr. John Gottman, a respected researcher whose work has received high acclaim, marriages that fail become infected with what he calls "the Four Horsemen." These four horsemen are criticism, contempt, defensiveness, and stonewalling (Gottman 1994, 1999).

Over time, as these four horsemen infiltrate a couple's exchanges, they undermine hope, trust, intimacy, love, and friendship, and they fill a marriage with toxic feelings and thoughts of hopelessness, anger, guilt, shame, and resentment. The end result is that couples who begin their relationship as soul mates drift apart and slowly feel more like roommates, and eventually even like cell mates. The remainder of this chapter will illustrate how these four horsemen negatively impact marital satisfaction and oneness, ultimately causing a marriage to fail.

Criticism

Criticism can be constructive or destructive. Constructive criticism is essentially good for marriage, whereas destructive criticism is very bad for marriages. Let me explain what I mean.

> CONSTRUCTIVE CRITICISM DOES NOT ATTACK THE OTHER PERSON.

Constructive criticism facilitates communication and helps couples address issues and problems that can create emotional distance and undermine marital satisfaction and oneness. Constructive criticism does not attack the other person; its focus is on an issue or problem that has the potential to undermine marital satisfaction and oneness.

Conversely, when destructive criticism is used, the issue or problem fades into the backdrop, and the recipient feels attacked. Unlike constructive criticism, destructive criticism typically involves insults, mild sarcasm, name-calling, and impatience. The following examples demonstrate both types of criticisms. They involve a fictional couple I will call Rhonda and Spiro. This couple is a composite of many couples with whom I have worked.

Constructive Criticism: More Cuddle Time and More Sex

It's been a year and a half since Rhonda and Spiro's wedding day, and their love life has begun to suffer. When they first married, they were making love two or more times a week. Over the past six months, the passion and frequency have decreased. Spiro has brought the subject up from time to time, but the issue remains unresolved and, by Spiro's standards, continues to remain unattended. As a result, Spiro decides to take a more proactive approach and states, "Rhonda, I'd like to talk to you about something important. Do you have any time today to talk?"

"Sure. What's up?"

Spiro smiles, gives his wife a kiss on her cheek, and says, "This may take some time, and maybe you're busy now."

"No, I'm not busy," Rhonda states. "Besides, you've got me curious, and I don't want to wait until later to find out what's bothering you. I can drop what I'm doing."

"Okay," Spiro says. Clearly a little nervous, Spiro continues, "But promise me you won't get upset."

"I promise I will try not to get upset."

"No," Spiro says. "Promise!"

"Okay, okay. So, what's up?"

A bit sheepishly, Spiro proceeds. "Well, I'd like to talk about our sex life."

"Hmm . . . our sex life. What about our sex life?" Rhonda half smiles but also appears a bit more serious.

"Okay, so this is hard for me because I don't what to upset you or hurt you, but it's no secret that we're not entirely happy with our sex life, and I'd like us to figure out how to improve it."

Rhonda looks a bit unsettled and states, "Okay . . . go on."

"Well, I would like to be with you more."

"So, you want more sex!" Rhonda snaps back.

"Well, yes, but that's not all I want. I also want us to be with one another more."

Rhonda softens and states, "That's what I also want."

The couple spends the next hour talking about their sex life from each partner's perspective.

The end result is that they come up with a plan that can be summarized in a few words: more cuddle time and more sex.

Constructive Criticism: More Couple Time and Some Buddy Time

Six months after this exchange, Rhonda is feeling unsettled because Spiro has been going out with his friends more and is spending less time at home with her. At first, she casually mentions this to Spiro, and he listens and even seems to agree with her. However, his amount of buddy time does not significantly decrease. As a result, Rhonda decides to take a more proactive approach.

"Spiro, I think we need to talk."

"Okay, what's up, babe?"

"Well, I'm a little upset," Rhonda states.

"Really? Upset about what?"

"Well, you've been spending more and more time with your friends and less time at home. Anyway, I miss you, and I guess I'm a bit jealous."

"Okay. But that doesn't mean I don't like spending time with you. You're absolutely my favorite person in the whole world, and I really like spending time with you, but sometimes I need some time with my buddies."

"I understand your need to do guy stuff, but that's not enough for me," Rhonda tearfully states.

On the heels of that disclosure, the couple enters into a discussion, which leads to some mutually satisfying decisions. Their decisions can be summed up as follows: more couple time and some buddy time.

SUMMARY STATEMENT

In both instances, each partner refrained from attacking the other and remained focused on enhancing couple intimacy and couple time. The end result is that this couple was able to partner together and find some mutually satisfying resolutions to otherwise potentially explosive issues that create distance and conflict for many couples. Furthermore, the criticisms of each partner facilitated conversation that helped resolve lingering, potentially damaging issues and cultivated increased oneness.

Destructive Criticism

Six months later, Spiro is feeling increasingly frustrated with his and Rhonda's sex life. It seems they have slipped back into their old patterns, and their love-making is less passionate and more infrequent. As the couple is getting ready for bed, he's ruminating over what's occurred and concludes to himself, "It's been nearly three weeks since we made love, and there is no hint that she cares. That's unacceptable! I can't live like this. I've got to do something!" Here's how he chooses to broach the issue.

"So, ahh . . . when's the last time you thought about making love?" *(mild sarcasm)*

Rhonda is tired and is slightly irritated by this comment, but she tries not to show it, hoping he'll drop the subject and they can go to bed. Noticing that he's waiting for an answer, she states, "Spiro, it's late. I have a long day tomorrow. Can't we discuss this another time?"

Spiro is unwilling to budge and states, "It's always 'late' when it comes to this subject! Do you realize it's been nearly three weeks, and you don't seem to care if another three weeks pass before we make love?" *(impatience and an insult)*

"I said I'm not going to do this now! I need to get some sleep. I've got a big day tomorrow. Why do you always have to bring this up at eleven o'clock at night?" *(impatience)*

"Like I said, no time seems like a good time for you when it comes to this subject." *(insult, mild sarcasm, and impatience)*

"I've told you, if you'd just be more affectionate, maybe things would change. Why can't you get that! Are you that dense?" *(insult, mild sarcasm, name-calling, and impatience)*

"Don't make this into my problem! This isn't my problem. You can be so cold, selfish, and stubborn sometimes!" *(insult, mild sarcasm, name-calling, and impatience)*

The couple continues this type of exchange for the next forty minutes. Nothing is resolved.

They go to bed angry and don't speak for several days. Bad habits begin to enter their relationship.

Destructive Criticism: More Buddy Time and Less Couple Time

After the couple's first conversation regarding more couple time and less buddy time, Spiro made some changes and was spending more time at home. However, when the issue of the couple's sex life resurfaced and remained unresolved, he became less cooperative and began to spend more time away from home. This has not gone unnoticed.

One Friday evening, as Spiro is getting ready to go out and watch a play-off game with his friends, Rhonda curtly asks, "Where are you going?" *(impatience)*

"What? I told you on Monday that a few of us were going over Frank's house to watch the game tonight." *(impatience)*

"No . . . you told me you might go over to Frank's. That's a lot different from what you just said." *(more impatience and some sarcasm)*

"Don't tell me what I said! I know what I said! Anyway, what's the big deal?" *(more impatience and some sarcasm)*

"The big deal is that you told me you were going to start spending more time at home." *(insult, more impatience, and some sarcasm)*

This exchange triggers a thirty-minute argument, which leads to more recriminations and no mutually satisfying resolutions. Spiro eventually leaves the house frustrated and goes to Frank's. When he gets home, Rhonda is sleeping. They don't talk about this again. They remain angry for days. More bad habits begin to form.

SUMMARY STATEMENT

Once again, the reason why these exchanges are examples of destructive criticism is because both partners lose sight of the problem—their sex life and more couple time—and they attack one another. Moreover, the personal and ugly nature of their remarks creates emotional distance and undermines marital oneness.

Contempt

If enough destructive criticism enters a couple's exchanges, the second horseman, contempt, will soon appear. In the simplest of terms, contempt is a heightened form of criticism. Typically, along with sarcasm, name-calling, and impatience, couples' exchanges include biting insults, threats, more shouting, liberal doses of hateful profanity, and palpable levels of impatience. Here are two examples of what contempt looks and sounds like.

Contempt and Less Sex

It's been almost two months since Rhonda and Spiro have been intimate. The couple is watching a movie, which includes a highly charged sex scene.

"Now there's a lucky guy," Spiro states. *(sarcasm and a veiled insult)*

Rhonda retorts. "What's that mean?" *(impatience)*

"It means that he's a lucky guy and I'm not!" *(some shouting, more sarcasm, and a biting insult)*

At this point, the couple forgets about the movie and becomes absorbed in an ugly exchange of words.

"I've told you, Mr. Romance, that you've got to change. But no, Mr. Ro-

> ### CONTEMPT IS A HEIGHTENED FORM OF CRITICISM.

mance hasn't listened. You dope, now you've ruined the movie for me!" *(more shouting, biting insults)*

"You can be such a mean @#*!" *(profanity, a biting insult, shouting)*

"You're such a jerk! If I had known the type of jerk you can be, I might have considered other options." (threat, biting insult, profanity)

Spiro and Rhonda become embroiled in a similar exchange that lasts for over an hour. Spiro sleeps on the couch. For the first time, he wonders what life might be like without Rhonda. They never revisit this argument. Bad habits continue to form.

Contempt and More Buddy Time

A few weeks later, Spiro is getting ready to leave the house. Rhonda curtly asks him, "What are you doing?"

Spiro reacts with the following statement. "What's it look like I'm doing? I'm getting ready to go over to Sam's house. Anyway, what do you care? You hardly ever show me any attention!" *(biting insult, some shouting, palpable levels of impatience)*

"Oh, you mean sex, right!" (sarcasm, shouting, biting insult, impatience)

"You're such a %#%@." (hateful profanity, palpable levels of impatience)

"Yeah, well, Mr. Foul-Mouth, keep it up. That'll get you nowhere in the sex department." *(sarcasm, name-calling, more shouting, palpable levels of impatience)*

"Like I said, you can be such a cold @#%." *(hateful profanity, palpable levels of impatience)*

"Brilliant!" *(biting insult)*

The exchange continues for twenty minutes. Each partner's remarks are filled with lots of sarcasm, name-calling, impatience, biting insults, threats, shouting, liberal amounts of hateful profanity, and palpable levels of impatience. Spiro eventually just leaves. When he returns, he sleeps on the coach. The couple does not speak for days. They never revisit the argument. Bad habits continue to form.

Defensiveness

As more and more criticism and contempt fill a couple's exchanges, the third horseman, defensiveness, will soon appear. Partners become defensive to protect themselves from the other partner's attacks and from the pain that is associated with his or her attacks. Unfortunately, defensiveness also creates walls between partners by blocking connection and undermining oneness. This is what defensiveness sounds like.

Spiro: "The only reason you want me to spend more time at home is so that you can control me more."

Rhonda: "Oh, that's so insightful! It's comments like these that are pushing me away."

Spiro: "Yeah, yeah. It's always my fault. For once I'd like you to make a statement that includes your faults."

Rhonda: "And you're not guilty?"

> DEFENSIVENESS . . . CREATES WALLS BETWEEN PARTNERS BY BLOCKING CONNECTION AND UNDERMINING ONENESS.

Spiro: "At least my statements are balanced! I admit to my faults!"

Rhonda: "Yeah, sure, I can count those attempts on one finger."

Spiro: "You're such a $#%&."

Rhonda: "There's Mr. Foul-Mouth again."

Spiro: "There's Ms. Perfect—it's never my fault."

Stonewalling

As these three horsemen become more and more pronounced in a couple's exchanges, eventually one partner—often the husband—will shut down, tune out, and turn away from his or her spouse. This is when the fourth horseman, stonewalling, usually shows up. Moreover, the reason why one partner will stonewall is because he or she is sick of being attacked and doesn't know how to respond any more for fear he or she will say the wrong thing or do something he or she might regret, like become verbally or physically abusive. So, he or she will shut down, tune out, and turn away.

When this happens, the couple will continue to drift apart. Moreover, sooner or later one of the two partners will consult a divorce lawyer—generally without the other partner's knowledge.

Other Predictable Consequences

Some five years into their relationship, Rhonda and Spiro's exchanges are saturated with the four horsemen, impacting their relationship in the following predictable ways:

- Emotional and physical intimacy is seriously compromised, and both partners will likely state that their sex life is suffering or nonexistent.

- Trust has waned, and both partners will tend to misinterpret each other's motives, often thinking the worst of one another.

- Commitment to the relationship has all but dissipated, and the "d-word" (divorce) has likely been used numerous times. In most cases, one or both partners have likely spent considerable time thinking about what life might be like without the other partner.

> [STONEWALLING OCCURS WHEN PARTNERS] SHUT DOWN, TUNE OUT, AND TURN AWAY.

- Empathy has also disappeared, and neither partner is likely able to feel the other partner's pains and frustrations because both partners are too busy defending themselves and justifying their thoughts and actions.

- Their private thoughts are saturated with negativity—they think the worst of their partner and seriously question the viability of their marriage.

- Both partners also begin feeling more and more like innocent victims in the aftermath of their regular painfully destructive exchanges.

- Both partners are also feeling righteous indignation or feelings and thoughts that serve to justify their anger and resentment.

- By this time friendship has eroded, and the warm fuzzies they experienced early in their relationship have been replaced with prickly feelings.

- The fun is lost, the thrill is gone, and the sizzle has long since fizzled. In short, if their relationship could be compared to a bank account, this couple's marriage is bankrupt.

What Can I Do If I Relate to the Above?

If physical abuse, drug abuse, chronic forms of gambling, and other forms of serious abusive behavior are absent, research indicates that it is possible for you to reclaim marital satisfaction (Amato and Booth 1997). However, you should also know that such an effort will not be easy. With God's help and guidance, your mutual commitment to change, your pastor's support, and a good marriage-friendly therapist, you can slowly but surely remove the horsemen in your marriage and reverse course so that you can reclaim what you have both lost.

Questions for Reflection

1. How many of these four horsemen are in our marriage?

2. What am I contributing to the difficulties in my marriage?

3. What is God's will for our marriage?

4. What qualities does my partner have that attracted me to him or her?

5. If children are involved, shouldn't we try couples counseling for the children's sake?

RECOMMENDED READING

- *A Generation at Risk: Growing Up in an Era of Family Upheaval.* Amato, P., and A. Booth. 1997. Cambridge, MA: Harvard University Press.

- *The Five Love Languages: How to Express Heartfelt Commitment to Your Mate.* Chapman, G. 2004. Chicago: Northfield Publishing.

- *Take Back Your Marriage: Sticking Together in a World That Pulls Us Apart.* Doherty, W. J. 2001. New York: Guilford Press.

- *Why Marriages Succeed or Fail.* Gottman, J. 1994. New York: Simon and Schuster.

- *The Seven Principles for Making Marriage Work.* Gottman, J. M., and N. Silver. 1999. New York: Three Rivers Press.

- *Attending to Your Marriage: A Resource for Christian Couples.* Joanides, C. 2006. Minneapolis, MN: Light & Life Publishing.

- *How to Improve Your Marriage without Talking about It.* Love, P., and S. Stosney. 2007. New York: Broadway Books.

- *Fighting for Your Marriage.* Markman, H., and S. Stanley. 2010. Revised edition. San Francisco: Jossey-Bass Publishers.

- *A Lasting Promise: A Christian Guide to Fighting for Your Marriage.* Stanley, S., D. Tratheon, S. McCain, and M. Bryan. 1998. San Francisco: Jossey-Bass Publishers.

HELPFUL WEBSITES

www.marriagefriendlytherapists.com

www.aamft.org

www.smartmarriages.com

MYTHS ABOUT DIVORCE

*"Finally, brethren, whatever is true, whatever is honorable, whatever is just,
whatever is pure, whatever is lovely, whatever is gracious, if there is any
excellence, if there is anything worthy of praise, think about these things."*
—Philippians 4:8

Lou (44) and Jennifer (37) have entered therapy to decide if they will divorce. Both deny the presence of spousal abuse, infidelity, drug and alcohol abuse, and other similar destructive behaviors in their marriage. Both also state that they have been emotionally disconnected and mildly conflicted for several years. They have two children, John (6) and Abby (11). When Jennifer is asked for her thoughts about the marriage, she states, "Truthfully, I've been seriously thinking about moving on. I've been so unhappy and unfulfilled for a very long time, and it doesn't appear as though things will ever get better. But there's also a part of me that makes me feel a bit guilty about what I'm thinking. Despite the guilt, I feel like I owe it to myself to move on to a happier place because I don't think things will ever change between us." Once Jennifer finishes, Lou adds the following: "I'm a little more committed to the marriage and might like to save it, but I don't see how that's possible if Jen isn't interested. Anyway, I suspect it won't be a big deal if we divorce. We'll get attorneys, and in a year or so it'll be over and we can both start fresh." When asked how they think their children will fare, both parents state, "We don't believe it will be a big deal for them. With our help and support, they will get over it."

How accurate are Lou's and Jennifer's statements about divorce?

The truth is, not very accurate. The best research indicates that divorce takes a toll on all members of a family—especially on the children. When children are involved divorce doesn't end the relationship between two conflicted spouses; it often complicates that relationship and the relationship of the spouses with their children. After a divorce parents must retain some connection with each other—a connection that is often strained and conflicted—for the sake of the children, and this often puts the children in a difficult position. Then, when ex-spouses remarry, as 70% of divorced persons do, the situation becomes more complicated; the

> DIVORCE TAKES A TOLL ON ALL MEMBERS OF A FAMILY—ESPECIALLY ON THE CHILDREN.

emotional pain of family members is further compounded as the new challenges of mixed allegiances to children from the first and second marriages emerge.

Those Who Buy into Myths

Lou and Jennifer have bought into certain myths about divorce that pervade our society yet have no empirical support. They are not alone. Experts maintain that most of us are influenced by similar myths, and that a sizeable percentage of couples who seek a divorce are like Lou and Jennifer.

Given some of the pervading myths about marriage, this chapter is offered to counterbalance the misinformation we have absorbed by living in a culture that finds divorce socially acceptable. Furthermore, it is written for couples like Jennifer and Lou who are contemplating a divorce. If you are contemplating divorce, hopefully what follows will cause you to rethink this option and only consider divorce as a last resort, after all other options have been carefully considered and eliminated.

Four Common Myths about Marriage and Divorce

Myth #1: When spouses are unhappy it is better for all family members if they divorce.

Many of us have heard variations of this statement. Yet a number of reliable and valid studies have shown that when low-conflict couples like Jennifer and Lou choose to divorce, all family members—especially the children—are prone to suffering negative, toxic, long-lasting consequences. The following statements, which are based on sound research, reinforce the toxic impact of divorce on all family members:

- "Marital dissatisfaction is probably not in and of itself psychologically damaging for children: what counts is whether, how often, and how intensely parents fight in front of their children. . . . When it comes to helping children succeed in school, the structural benefits of marriage—more money, better schools and neighborhoods, and more time for supervision—seem to matter more than whether or not parents have a close and warm marital relationship." *–The Case for Marriage, pp. 144–45*

- "Divorce ... increase[s] poverty for children and mothers ... between one-fifth and one-third of divorcing women end up in poverty following the divorce." *–Why Marriage Matters, p. 23*

- "Married people, especially married men, have longer life expectancies than do otherwise similar singles. . . . In most developed countries, middle-aged . . . divorced . . . men are about twice as likely to die as married men." *–Why Marriage Matters, p. 30*

- "Marriage is associated with better health and lower rates of injury, illness, and disability for both men and women." *—Why Marriage Matters, p. 31*

Myth #2: It's better to divorce than to endure a lifetime of unhappiness.

Quotes such as "Be good to yourself" and "You deserve better" seem to pervade in our society and encourage conflicted spouses to consider their individual needs above the needs of the children and family. Along with these catchphrases, spouses like Irene, a 45-year-old attorney who came to me considering divorce, illustrate how this myth infiltrates our thinking and distorts our perspective. "I'm still young. I feel like I have a lot to offer someone—especially myself. I could be stuck in this bland lifestyle forever. I can't accept that. I've got to do something about this now before too much time passes. Before I know it, I'll be fifty!"

Despite the individualistic, "me-first" values that undergird these and other similar catchphrases and comments, researchers have discovered that many unhappy, conflicted marriages have the potential to become happy, life-giving marriages when couples are invested in and willing to do the hard work of reclaiming the intimacy and love they have lost. These efforts will protect them and their children from the long-term toxic effects of divorce. If you are considering divorce, please consider the following research finding:

> MANY UNHAPPY, CONFLICTED MARRIAGES HAVE THE POTENTIAL TO BECOME HAPPY, LIFE-GIVING MARRIAGES WHEN COUPLES ARE INVESTED IN AND WILLING TO DO THE HARD WORK OF RECLAIMING THE INTIMACY AND LOVE THEY HAVE LOST.

- "Even the unhappiest of couples who grimly stick it out for the sake of the children can find happiness together a few years down the road. . . . 86% of unhappily married people who stick it out find that, five years later, their marriages are happier." *–The Case for Marriage, p. 142*

Myth #3: If parents are conflicted, children will be better off if the parents divorce.

"We just aren't getting along," stated Samuel, who was seeing me to decide if he would pursue a divorce. "We don't do much together, and we typically seem irritated with one another. In fact, I often wonder what kind of a toll our unhappy marriage is having on the kids. Lately I've thought about divorce. I've also thought it might be the best thing for all of us—kids included." As Samuel's comments suggest, this myth may serve to as-

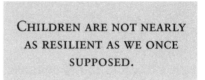

Children are not nearly as resilient as we once supposed.

suage the guilt of a parent who is contemplating divorce, but can Samuel's fears and concerns regarding his children's well-being be justified? Once again, the answer to this question is a resounding "no."

Longitudinal studies examining the effects of divorce on children maintain that—unless there is evidence of chronic and serious abuse or some other destructive behavior—children are better off if their parents do not divorce. Research results also affirm that children are not nearly as resilient as we once supposed and that divorce has numerous negative effects that extend into adulthood. The following statements validate these points:

- "Children who live with their own two married parents enjoy better physical health, on average, than do children in other family forms." –*Why Marriage Matters, p. 28*

- "Our parents' divorce is linked to our higher rates of depression, suicidal attempts and thoughts, health problems, childhood sexual abuse, school dropout, failure to attend college, arrests, addiction, teen pregnancy, and more. . . . We have a harder time finishing school, getting and keeping jobs, maintaining relationships, and having lasting marriages." –*Between Two Worlds: The Inner Lives of Children of Divorce, p. 189*

- "The idea of the 'good divorce' bears little resemblance to children's reality. Even in a 'good divorce,' half of us say we always felt like adults, even as little kids. Half say our family lives were stressful. More than half say they experienced many losses. Close to half say our parents' household rules were different. Almost a third say our versions of the truth were different. A third say we were alone a lot as children . . . the stories of children of divorce show that it is wrong and misleading to describe our experience as 'good.'" –*Between Two Worlds, p. 171*

- "A central finding in my research is that children identify not only with their mother and father as separate individuals but with the relationship between them. They carry the template of this relationship into adulthood and use it to seek the image of their new family. The absence of a good image negatively influences their search for love, intimacy, and commitment. Anxiety leads many into making bad choices in relationships, giving up hastily when problems arise, or avoiding relationships altogether." *–The Unexpected Legacy of Divorce, p. xxix*

Myth #4: Fathers can be replaced.

Nichole (34) and Frank (40) are in couples therapy. Frank wants to save the marriage, but Nichole is leaning toward divorce. Frank is a captain in the army. In two months he will be deployed to the Middle East for the second time in four years. Nichole appears distraught and clearly weary of military life as Frank speaks of his pending assignment. At the same time, she confesses to some guilt and also admits she is having some serious mixed feelings about the future of their marriage. To complicate matters, the couple has a three-year-old, and they are expecting their second child four months from now. During an individual session she shares the following observation: "If we get divorced, I'll probably move back home. I've got two brothers and a father. I know it's not exactly the same, but our child will be okay. Besides, Frank is hardly around when he's not in some other part of the world. Our child will be alright."

Nichole's beliefs are misguided. The best research suggests that fathers have an invaluable, positive impact on their children and families. The following general observations from research support this assertion.

- "Hundreds of studies over the past two decades have consistently demonstrated that fathers have a measurable impact on children." *–Do Fathers Matter Uniquely for Adolescent Well-Being?*

- "Mothers and fathers both make vital contributions to adolescent well-being. In a few instances, fathers and mothers appear to be interchangeable. There are more instances, however, in which mothers and fathers complement each other in their characteristics or behavior in ways that benefit children, and in most cases fathers make positive contributions to the well-being of their children beyond what mothers do." *–Do Fathers Matter Uniquely for Adolescent Well-Being?*

- "In today's dominant cultural conversation, probably the central prescription regarding fatherhood is to lower our standards.... Instead of good fathers, we settle for child-support payments." *–Fatherless America, p. 211*

- "If mothers are likely to devote special attention to their children's present physical and emotional needs, fathers are likely to devote special attention to character traits necessary for the future, especially qualities such as independence, self-reliance, and the willingness to test limits and take risks. If mothers frequently set the standards for children's conduct within the home, fathers often take special interest and pride in their children's conduct outside the home. When asked to define the satisfaction of parenthood, mothers are likely to describe the qualities of the mother-child bond. But fathers, much more frequently than mothers, link parental satisfaction directly to successful outcomes for their children in the society." *–Fatherless America, p. 218*

- "A father plays a distinctive role in shaping a daughter's sexual style and her understanding of the male-female bond. A father's love and involvement builds a daughter's confidence in her femininity and contributes to her sense that she is worth loving. This sense of love-worthiness gives young women a greater sense of autonomy and independence in later relationships with men. Consequently, women who have good relationships with their fathers are less likely to engage in an anxious quest for male approval or seek male affection through promiscuous sexual behavior." *–Fatherless America, p. 46*

- "For boys, the most socially acute manifestation of paternal disinvestments is juvenile violence. For girls, it is juvenile and out-of-wedlock childbearing. One primary result of growing fatherlessness is more boys with guns and more girls with babies." *–Fatherless America, p. 45*

A Few Final Thoughts

Research indicates that many low-conflict couples who choose divorce do so because they believe that divorce is a solution to their problems. In some cases where there is evidence of destructive behavior—such as serious and chronic physical abuse, repeated substance abuse, or another destructive form of behavior—divorce may well be the best option. However, when such behaviors are not present, a growing body of valid and reliable research studies suggests that divorce is not the best option for couples, and especially not for children. In these cases research suggests that couples considering divorce may be better served if they consider outside help.

> "86% OF UNHAPPILY MARRIED PEOPLE WHO STICK IT OUT FIND THAT, FIVE YEARS LATER, THEIR MARRIAGES ARE HAPPIER."

If you are presently in a low-conflict marriage and have been considering divorce, I urge you, based on the information in this chapter and the next chapter, to reconsider this option and find some outside help. Often, a good way to begin your search for help is to consult your pastor. If your pastor is unable to help, then you should consider finding a marriage-friendly therapist in your area. The following two websites can be helpful in your search: www.aamft.org/ and www.marriagefriendlytherapists.com.

Chances are that your opinions about your marriage have been shaped by the myths featured in this chapter and that outside help from a marriage-friendly professional can provide more balance— balance that can reinvigorate your marriage and help you reclaim the love and intimacy that have been lost.

Questions for Reflection

- What myths about divorce have you bought into?

- How have these myths influenced your understanding of marriage?

- If you are contemplating divorce, what in this chapter might give you pause, and how will you consider the possibility of changing course?

RECOMMENDED READING

- *Reconcilable Differences.* Christensen, A., and N. S. Jacobson. 2000. New York: Guilford.

- *The State of Our Unions 2006: The Social Health of Marriage in America,* pp. 1–44. Dafoe Whitehead, B., and D. Popenoe. 2006. http://marriage.rutgers.edu/Publications/Print?PrintSOOU2006.htm.

- *Do Fathers Matter Uniquely for Adolescent Well-Being?* Eggebeen, D. 2008. Research Brief No. 14. New York: Institute for American Values.

- *Attending to Your Marriage: A Resource for Christian Couples.* Joanides, C. 2006. Minneapolis, MN: Light and Life Publishing, 2006.

- *Fighting for Your Marriage.* Markman, H., S. Stanley, and S. Blumberg. 1994. San Francisco: Jossey-Bass Publishers.

- *Between Two Worlds: The Inner Lives of Children of Divorce.* Marquardt, E. 2005. New York: Crown Publishers.

- *Why Marriage Matters.* Institute for American Values and the National Marriage Project. 2011. 3rd ed. New York: Institute for American Values.

- *The Case for Marriage: Why Married People Are Happier, Healthier, and Better Off Financially.* Waite, Linda, and Maggie Gallagher. 2010. New York: Doubleday.

- *The Unexpected Legacy of Divorce: A 25 Year Landmark Study.* Wallerstein, J. S., J. M. Lewis, and S. Blakeslee. 2000. New York: Hyperion.

Rethinking Divorce:
Ten Strategies That Can Help

"I have held many things in my hands, and lost them all; but whatever I placed in God's hands, that I still possess." —*Saint Augustine*

Over the past few years, I've received several messages like the following one, from both men and women:

> Dear Father,
>
> I don't know why I'm writing you. I suppose I just felt a need to write someone. . . . It's been eight years since my divorce, but I'm still not certain I made the right choice. We were married for eleven years when we decided to end it. We had been growing apart for several years, and the only common commitment we had was to the children. . . . One day we started talking about our unhappy marriage. We both agreed we weren't happy. . . . When I look back, I think that conversation got us both thinking about divorce. . . . It wasn't long before the idea "to end it" grew into a serious consideration. . . . I started consulting friends and family to get their opinions. Most supported my thinking. . . . Before I knew it, attorneys were involved, and we were caught in a process that seemed impossible to reverse. . . . It's now been nearly eight years since my divorce and way down deep I still have some regrets and doubts. . . .
>
> –*E-mail respondent*

Such respondents speak with mixed feelings about their divorces. Some messages are more emotional than others. However, almost all describe a similar scenario unfolding. "We weren't happy when we decided to end it. . . . Friends and relatives supported my decision. . . . The idea grew into a serious consideration until it gained a momentum that seemed as if it couldn't be reversed. . . . It's been x number of years, and I still have regrets." When two people find themselves in an unhappy marriage, it's not long before they begin hearing messages such as: "You deserve more. . . . Life's too short. . . . If you're not happy, then maybe you should end it. . . . You have your whole life ahead of you. . . . You'll be okay. . . . The kids will get over it."

If You Are Having Marital Problems . . .

If you're having marital problems, you will likely be inundated with voices encouraging you to get out of the marriage. It is unlikely that you will hear with any regularity, "Don't give up. With God's help, it'll get better." So, please repeat these words each day at least ten times. When you repeat them, say them slowly and prayerfully, remembering that you are not alone and that God can help you.

Low to moderately conflicted couples who chose divorce as a solution to their problems tend to have three general emotional and cognitive responses: (1) mixed feelings, (2) regrets, and (3) a conviction that they have made a mistake. These thoughts and feelings are prompted by a variety of circumstances surrounding the divorce. For example, research indicates that the custodial parent may see his/her standard of living considerably compromised after a divorce. This drop in income undermines personal and family stability while also triggering toxic feelings and thoughts related to the divorce. Similarly, the non-custodial parent who no longer has easy access to his/her children may experience powerful noxious feelings and thoughts post divorce. And finally, children may silently grieve the loss of the non-custodial parent as well as the life they had before the divorce. As a result of these and numerous other negative outcomes associated with divorce, you owe it to yourselves and to your children to carefully and prayerfully consider the pros and cons of remaining married. The fact is, many low to moderately conflicted couples who attempt to repair their marriages successfully reclaim the happiness they've lost. Some even report more marital satisfaction than they have ever experienced.

Steps to Reclaim Your Marriage

Researchers now know what factors promote healthy marriages. This information has been used to develop counseling programs and strategies that can help two committed partners reclaim their marriages. However, the availability of effective counseling is not enough to save marriages. The best program, strategy, or counselor can only help a floundering marriage if both spouses are invested in and committed to the work and effort needed to reclaim their marriage. Many a time I have sat in a room with a spouse who simply couldn't find it in his or her heart to commit to therapy; thus, therapy failed.

> THE BEST PROGRAM, STRATEGY, OR COUNSELOR CAN ONLY HELP A FLOUNDERING MARRIAGE IF BOTH SPOUSES ARE INVESTED IN AND COMMITTED TO THE WORK AND EFFORT NEEDED TO RECLAIM THEIR MARRIAGES.

So, if you're currently in an unhappy relationship, do not give up. If you're interested in reclaiming the love, intimacy, and happiness that you've lost, please know that it's possible. With an unswerving, prayerful commitment to change, many couples can turn an unhappy marriage around. It will not be easy, but it is possible. I've seen it in my work with couples. Together with God's grace, the following suggestions may help you begin to reclaim your marriage.

1. Trust in God

Please remember that God wants to help you. He can help you reclaim the love and intimacy that compelled you to marry. The book of Proverbs states, "Trust in the Lord with all your heart, and do not rely on your own insight. In all your ways acknowledge Him, and He will make straight your paths" (3:5–6). Elsewhere, Jesus teaches, "For truly, I say to you, if you have faith as a grain of mustard seed, you will say to this mountain 'Move from here to there,' and it will move; and nothing will be impossible to you" (Matthew 17:20). So, trust in God and do your part; your chances of surviving the marital challenges you're currently encountering will improve.

2. God + Time + Cooperation = Wounds Healed

Be patient. If you continue to do your part, by making some changes and not giving in to the temptation to "end it," patience and time will strengthen your efforts to improve marital satisfaction. Remember that you've gotten where you presently find yourselves over the course of some time, and it will take time to reverse this process. Just as time heals other wounds, with God's help and your cooperation, time will heal your wounded marriage.

3. Agree to Place a Moratorium on Divorce-Talk

In your efforts to save your marriage, you will undoubtedly have certain setbacks. In fact, in the beginning you will sometimes feel like you are taking two steps forward and one step backward. When this happens, whether it is during the heat of battle over an unresolved lingering disagreement that raises its ugly head, or another circumstance that reminds you of your unhappiness, you may want to

> NOTHING UNDERMINES COUPLES' EFFORTS TO RECLAIM THEIR MARRIAGES MORE THAN DIVORCE-TALK.

talk about divorce, as many couples do. When emotions are heated, spouses in conflict may threaten divorce or decide to throw in the towel and consult an attorney.

Please be advised that if your mutual efforts to save your marriage from divorce are to succeed, you must agree to place a moratorium on ALL divorce-talk. Nothing undermines couples' efforts to reclaim their marriages more than divorce-talk. So, in your prayers ask God to help you avoid the "d" word.

4. Begin to Acknowledge Your Mistakes

When couples find themselves close to divorce, both spouses are apt to believe that the failing marriage is largely or exclusively their spouse's doing. However, that has not been my experience or the experience of professional marriage therapists. After working with hundreds of couples, I can tell you that both partners share responsibility for failing marriages, though the level of responsibility may not always be equal.

> WHEN YOU ARE STUCK IN A DIFFICULT PLACE, IT IS IMPORTANT TO SOMEHOW BROADEN YOUR PERSPECTIVE ON THE PROBLEMS AND UNDERSTAND THAT YOUR CONFLICTED MARRIAGE IS NOT "HIS FAULT" OR "HER FAULT."

Given the reality of shared responsibility on the part of both spouses, you would do well to examine how you've contributed to your marital problems and to take responsibility for your part. One way to do this is to set aside some private time to prayerfully develop a list of the things you've said and done, as well as the things you've failed to say and do, that have contributed to your marital woes. Then ask yourself how these words and actions have poisoned your marriage. If you do this exercise sincerely, and you're brutally honest with yourself, you'll be surprised at what you discover.

This exercise will not be easy to complete. However, it is a necessary beginning to turning things around in your marriage. When you are stuck in a difficult place, it is important to somehow broaden your perspective on the problems and understand that your conflicted marriage is not "his fault" or "her fault." Both of you have been negligent in caring for your marriage. The only way to begin resolving your problems is to stop pointing fingers at each other and to begin to point the finger at yourself first. Remember what Christ taught: "Judge not that you be not judged. . . . First take the log out of your own eye, and then you will see clearly to take the speck out of your brother's eye" (Matthew 7:1, 5).

5. Emphasize the Positive

If you are in a conflicted marriage, it has probably been a while since you complimented your spouse for anything or thought in positive terms about your marriage and spouse. In fact, it is most likely that your thoughts and feelings about your spouse and marriage are primarily negative. Negativity is very toxic to a relationship. But do you know how toxic? Researchers who study interpersonal relationships have concluded that for every negative interaction that occurs between two people, five positive interactions must occur to offset the negativity from the one negative interaction. What this means is that you'll need to work on infusing your relationship with warm-fuzzy thoughts and moments and start removing the prickly comments and behaviors that are slowly poisoning your marriage.

> FOR EVERY NEGATIVE INTERACTION THAT OCCURS BETWEEN TWO PEOPLE, FIVE POSITIVE INTERACTIONS MUST OCCUR TO OFFSET THE NEGATIVITY FROM THE ONE NEGATIVE INTERACTION.

6. Don't Just Think about Yourself

A "me-first" attitude—an attitude that emphasizes one's individual rights and needs while disregarding those of others—is often promoted in our society. Thus, we are inclined to think about ourselves first. However, in order to have a healthy marriage and family life, we must move away from thinking only about ourselves and our personal needs and instead balance them with what our marriage, children, and family need.

Often, when spouses are having problems, each is apt to think about his or her own needs almost exclusively. In the face of the disappointment, confusion, pain, and frustrations that they're experiencing, it's understandable that conflicted spouses focus on their personal needs. However, this is a skewed approach that invariably leads spouses toward marital meltdown and divorce.

The following comments from former clients illustrate this tendency to focus on personal needs:

- "I've been so unhappy. I just need to try something different."
- "Is it wrong to want more from life?"
- "She doesn't do it for me. I just don't know . . . I guess I need more."

The emphasis in these statements is on "I" and "me." Where is the concern for the marriages, families, and children of the people who made these comments? Why are these needs being ignored? Some people have good reasons to consider their personal needs and contemplate divorce. However, this self-centered thinking that is promoted by our culture sometimes compels people to think about divorce prematurely and with little thought or concern for the needs of others.

So, if you're on the road toward divorce or are contemplating the possibility of divorce, please look beyond your personal needs and also consider the needs of your marriage, family, and children, even if it is difficult to do this.

When you consider the needs of everyone who will be negatively impacted by a divorce, you may discover something that will help to turn things around.

Remember, all members of the family suffer when spouses divorce—especially children.

Thus, if there is any hope for reconciliation, you owe it to yourselves and your children to make an honest, prayerful effort at reclaiming the trust, understanding, intimacy, and love that's been lost.

7. What about God's Will?

In this complicated mix of contemplating divorce, many believers fail to permit God to participate in the decision-making process. Thus, please consider the following questions:

- To what extent do you believe divorce is God's will?
- On what basis can you justify your decision to seek a divorce?
- How do Holy Scripture and the Church support your decision to seek a divorce?

If you haven't bothered to ask these questions, please do so, even if you cannot answer them. While contemplating the questions, remember: God is not interested in keeping you in a destructive relationship, God wants the best for you, and God will not put you in harm's way or prevent you from finding happiness. In fact, He is profoundly interested in your well-being and happiness. So, invite Him into any thoughts you have regarding divorce and seek His will. Scripture teaches, "But seek first His kingdom and righteousness" (Matthew 6:33), and so He will guide and direct you to the appropriate answers for the hard questions you are asking.

8. Consult Your Priest

Research suggests that most conflicted spouses and couples connected to a faith community are likely to consult their pastor for help in resolving marital problems. Depending on how seriously you are conflicted, the counseling skills of many clergy and their pastoral expertise can prove helpful. In cases where complicating factors are present, such as depression, violence, or some other mental health issue, it may be best to consult a pro-marriage therapist first, because psychotherapists are trained to detect and work with these complicating factors. Should you decide to seek professional help, enlist your priest's help, because spiritual counseling, confession, and the sacraments are indispensable to your mutual efforts to revitalize your marriage and increase marital satisfaction.

9. Find a Competent Pro-Marriage Couples Therapist

Finding a pro-marriage couples therapist may be challenging because many psychotherapists who market themselves as marriage and couples therapists are more likely to focus on individual needs to the detriment of the marriage. Additionally, some therapists may disrespect or not understand a couple's religious orientation. Thus, you will need to spend some quality time in search of a pro-marriage therapist who has experience working with religious populations. In an effort to assist you with this challenge, here are a few suggestions.

- Approach your priest for a referral. He may provide you with the name of a professional pro-marriage therapist he knows and respects. Further, by approaching your pastor, you will begin to build a team to help you address your marital difficulties.

- If your priest does not have a referral, you can log on to one or both of the following websites: www.aamft.org. or www.marriagefriendlytherapists.com. Both have therapist locators that will help you identify therapists in your area. After you identify possible therapists, you can visit their websites and read their profiles.

- Look for therapists who specialize in couples' problems, have worked successfully with religious populations, and have a pro-marriage orientation. What is a therapist with a "pro-marriage orientation"? This is a therapist who makes the marriage the identified patient and focuses on the marriage's needs, while not ignoring each spouse's individual needs. A pro-marriage therapist will promote marital well-being, with an underlying assumption that marital well-being enhances personal well-being. In other words, seek a systems therapist.

- In your search to find a pro-marriage therapist, the following questions may be helpful. If the therapist does not address them or resists a paid initial consultation, then it is best to continue your search. These questions can be posed either on the telephone during an intake or in person at a paid consultation: What percentage of your work is with couples? What percentage of couples with whom you've worked would say they experienced a "positive" outcome? Do you work with religious populations? Do you feel you can be respectful to my religious perspective? Which approach do you take in therapy—more proactive or more observant?

- Share what you have discovered with your spouse. If you are both comfortable with the therapist's responses to your questions and you have reason to believe that the therapist will have a more proactive approach to therapy, make an initial appointment.

- After two or three sessions, you should begin to feel some relief and notice some signs of positive change or a new sense of hope for the relationship. If not, consider looking for another therapist.

- Keep in mind that many insurance companies do not generally cover couples therapy, so you may need to be prepared to pay out-of-pocket. Some therapists provide a sliding scale to make therapy more affordable.

10. If Your Spouse Refuses to Cooperate . . .

I've met many spouses who've said, "My husband doesn't think we have a problem, so he refuses to come to therapy," or "My wife thinks it's my problem and that I need therapy." Often, the spouse talking is also the one who's working overtime to save his or her marriage. The spouse looking for help has usually pleaded, cajoled, threatened, and relentlessly pursued his or her spouse to get help. However, all efforts have failed, and matters may have worsened. This spouse is usually exasperated, worn out, and experiencing some symptoms of depression. If you can relate to this description, don't throw up your hands in despair, thinking there's no hope. Instead, read the following strategies thoughtfully; they may be helpful.

- Stop pursuing your partner; the more you pursue, the more he or she will distance himself or herself from you. This pattern simply makes matters worse.

- Start taking care of yourself. Get a physical. Obtain some medication for the anxiety and depression, if warranted.

- Start exercising. Physical exercise is a great release.

- Begin praying, reading from Scripture, and receiving the sacraments regularly. In your prayers and Bible study, ask God to help you.

- Start working on living your life to its fullest, with or without your spouse. In most cases, this will mean you will begin living your life without your spouse. Cultivate old friendships and consider doing something you've wanted to do for a long time but have been too preoccupied to start because of your marital problems. In short, take all the energy you've been expending in promoting marital satisfaction, and channel it into the direction of personal well-being.

As confusing and contradictory as the thought of personal well-being may seem right now, it is best for you and may help your marriage. Before exploring the importance of personal well-being in the midst of serious marital problems, please take a moment to honestly answer the following question: Isn't it true that much of what you've tried to do to get your spouse to work on your marriage has failed? If so, then doing more of the same won't help. So, for the sake of your marriage, stop doing everything that hasn't worked.

The energy spouses expend trying to resolve marital problems often results in emotional difficulties, such as depression, anxiety, fears, and so on. If the spouses do not make changes, more emotional turmoil and sadness arise. So, start taking care of yourself; if you do, don't be surprised if your partner begins to take notice of your newly found positive attitude.

Self-care may produce several positive outcomes. It may reduce the tension between you and your spouse and provide both of you with some needed breathing room. It will also help you become more healthy, both physically and emotionally, thus increasing your ability to think more clearly and make sound decisions. Finally, if your partner is resolved to divorce you and the marriage comes to an end, you will be in a better position to move on with your life.

Some Marriages Die

Even the most admirable of efforts to reclaim your marriage can lead to divorce if your spouse is determined to end the marriage. In this case, there is little you can do, other than to accept the inevitable and move on. Ending a marriage is not easy, especially if you desperately want the marriage to succeed.

I've worked with numerous people who were unable to let go of their marriages. In a particular circumstance, one spouse was willing to overlook repeated promiscuous behavior, emotional abuse, and even occasional physical abuse. Despite urging from her closest relatives and friends—even her in-laws—to end the marriage, this sweet soul continued to endure the abuses, convinced it was God's will. Eventually she accepted the reality of her marriage and moved on, and she is now in a much better place. It took time, prayer, and therapy to help her see things more clearly.

Sometimes things just simply don't work out, and marriages die. If you're caught in a marriage that you've tried to keep together with no assistance from your spouse, remember that it takes two committed spouses to make a marriage. So, after you've done everything you can, if your spouse continues his or her abusive, insensitive ways, then—at the very minimum—it's time to talk to your pastor or a professional to gain a clearer perspective.

Conclusion

When you married, you and your spouse began coauthoring a book, a book about two people who chose to form a life together. If you've identified with this chapter's contents, then several of the recent chapters you've coauthored may not be much fun to review. However, that doesn't mean you have to continue writing chapters filled with conflict and heartache, or that the only way to stop writing painful chapters is to divorce your spouse. You have another option.

Decide to commit yourselves to revitalizing your marriage for the next six to eight months, and make your marriage a top priority. If you utilize the materials outlined in this chapter, seek God's guidance through prayer and your pastor, and pursue professional help, you may successfully revitalize your marriage, experience increased marital satisfaction, and coauthor a book about two people who, by God's grace and their cooperation, make a beautiful life together.

Questions for Reflection

• What is your attitude toward divorce?

• What are the voices around you telling you to do about your marriage?

• If you are having marital problems, what are you willing to do to reclaim your marriage?

• Which of the steps described in this chapter have you taken to reclaim your marriage, and which do you still need to take?

• How do you know if your marriage is over?

RECOMMENDED READING

• *Reconcilable Differences.* Christensen, A., and N. Jacobson. 1999. New York: Guilford Press.

• *Divorce Culture: Rethinking Our Commitments to Marriage and Family.* Dafoe Whitehead, B. 1996. New York: Vintage Books.

• *The Seven Principles for Making Marriage Work.* Gottman, J. M., and N. Silver. 1999. New York: Three Rivers Press.

• *Attending to Your Marriage: A Resource for Christian Couples.* Joanides, C. Minneapolis, MN: Light & Life Publishing.

• *When You Intermarry: A Resource for Inter-Christian, Intercultural Couples, Parents and Families.* Joanides, C. 2002. New York: Greek Orthodox Archdiocese of America.

• *Fighting for Your Marriage.* Markman, H., S. Stanley, and S. Blumberg. 1994. San Francisco. Jossey-Bass Publishers.

• *Rekindling Desire: A Step-by-Step Program to Help Low-Sex and No-Sex Marriages.* McCarthy, B., and E. McCarthy. 2003. New York: Brunner-Routledge.

• *A Lasting Promise: A Christian Guide to Fighting for Your Marriage.* Stanley, S., D. Tratheon, S. McCain, and M. Bryan. 1998. San Francisco: Jossey-Bass Publishers.

• *Divorce Remedy.* Weiner-Davis, M. 2001. New York: Simon & Schuster.

MONEY MATTERS: HOW FINANCES IMPACT MARRIAGE AND DIVORCE

"For the love of money is the root of all evils; it is through this craving that some have wandered away from the faith and pierced their hearts with many pangs." –1 Timothy 6:10

Flawed and failed financial strategies either create problems for couples or exacerbate existing issues and difficulties (Wilcox, Marquardt, and Popenoe 2009). Results from numerous research studies reinforce these points and suggest that regular couple disagreements related to finances are a good predictor of separation and divorce (Wilcox, Marquardt, and Popenoe 2009; Dakin and Wampler 2008; Conger et al. 1990). Conducting an honest self-evaluation of your financial practices and making some corrections can help couples isolate and remove some of the differences, difficulties, and disappointments that are contributing to serious marital discord (Wilcox, Marquardt, and Popenoe 2009). This chapter can help you achieve this objective.

> FLAWED AND FAILED FINANCIAL STRATEGIES EITHER CREATE PROBLEMS FOR COUPLES OR EXACERBATE EXISTING ISSUES AND DIFFICULTIES.

Money Matters and Marital Discord

I have worked with many conflicted spouses and couples whose attitudes related to money undermined their efforts to cultivate marital satisfaction and oneness. These individuals possessed little or no regard for their spouses' needs and perspectives, not to mention God's will.

One spouse hoarded substantial amounts of money from his wife and children. His justification for this behavior was: "I made it. It's mine." He provided his wife with a small allowance, which barely covered the household's needs, while leading her to believe that the family was one step away from being destitute. In another instance, a spouse regularly belittled her unemployed husband, reminding him that he was an inadequate protector and provider. These criticisms were very destructive and sabotaged this couple's efforts to cultivate connection and unity. Another couple with whom I worked carefully scrutinized each other's spending habits. Both spent inordinate amounts of time criticizing one another but were essentially blind to their own spending problems. Yet another spouse with whom I worked engaged in spending sprees. By the time I met with her and her husband, she had accumulated tens of thousands of dollars of credit card debt without her husband's knowledge. Her husband resorted to cutting up their credit cards. This did not stop her from secretly applying for other cards, which caused this couple to slip deeper into financial ruin. It is no surprise that in these cases the couples prematurely ended therapy and divorced.

> THE SKEWED, SELF-CENTERED ATTITUDES RELATED TO MONEY THAT SPOUSES AND COUPLES ADOPT SERVE TO CREATE AN UNBRIDGEABLE DIVIDE PARTNERS.

Financial strategies like these create irreparable damage to marriages. The skewed, self-centered attitudes related to money that spouses and couples adopt serve to create an unbridgeable divide between partners. Over time, trust, understanding, and intimacy are seriously compromised, irrevocably derailing a couple's efforts to build a life together.

Helpful Strategies

Other couples who acknowledged their spending problems and resolved to make some changes also come to mind. One couple who had taken out several loans against their home and maxed out their credit cards resolved to turn things around. Together with a financial planner, they placed themselves on a strict budget, began to attend couples therapy to help them partner more effectively, and were well on the way to being debt free when they terminated therapy. In another instance, two partners in their second marriage entered therapy to attend to numerous stepfamily adjustment issues. One year after their wedding, they were on the brink of another divorce. Money matters were often at the heart of these arguments. Specifically, each partner had a different opinion regarding the level of support they should be offering his young-adult sons, who were both in college. She believed his sons should assume the lion's share of responsibility for their college education and she and her husband should save the money for a new home and their future children. He believed he should pay half of his two sons' college tuition while also saving money for the couple's future well-being. After a number of very difficult sessions, the couple established a joint account for their future needs while also protecting college funds that had existed prior to their marriage. Another couple in their mid-thirties, who were considering filing for bankruptcy when therapy began, decided to place themselves on an austerity budget and were able to slowly but surely move beyond financial ruin. Once they took these and other crucial steps, the intensity of their arguments slowly abated, they stopped blaming one another, and they were able to partner together to surrender their debts. Two years after ending therapy, they sent me the following message attached to a Christmas card.

> Dear Father Charles,
>
> We thought you'd like to know that we are doing well. Our business is out of the red, we have joined a church, Bill attends a Christian men's support group, and I attend a young mothers' support group—yes, we're pregnant! God helped us find our way through the mess we were in when we first saw you. We remain on a strict budget and will be debt free in a few years. Thank you for believing in us and helping us to believe in ourselves.

Two years later I received another Christmas card, along with another update. Here is a small excerpt from the message that was included.

> Dear Father Charles,
>
> With much pride we can say we are finally in the black and are saving for our children's future—that's right, "children." We now have two beautiful children. God has been very gracious toward us. We continue to feel really blessed. Do we still have our share of problems? Yes. But now we walk with Christ and not alone. This has made all the difference in our lives. Christ is born, glorify Him.

You Can Do It

If you are currently experiencing serious marital problems and money matters are a recurring theme in your arguments, the following strategies may prove helpful. Compare the suggestions that follow with your present guiding principles and then spend some time answering the questions at the end of this chapter. Isolating some of the issues and problems you have in relation to your finances may prove helpful to you in your efforts to begin addressing the marital discord you and your partner are experiencing.

No Secrets

Secrets related to money matters are not compatible with marriage from a Christian perspective. This area of a couple's life should remain transparent. If one spouse has hidden assets or debts, no matter what the reason, these assets and debts eventually come to light and compromise trust and, by extension, a couple's efforts to develop oneness. A statement by one spouse with whom I met after a particularly ugly divorce illustrates how toxic secrets can be related to finances: "I should have told her about the child support I was paying before we married, but I didn't. When she found out, she couldn't get past this, and things were never quite the same. In retrospect, this was the beginning of the end of our marriage."

Talk and Share

Making the time to regularly and prayerfully stay in touch with one another is essential in a couple's efforts to avoid issues and problems related to money matters. The following observations illustrate how a lack of meaningful communication can compromise marital oneness. During couples therapy, out of frustration one spouse stated, "She does the banking, and that's okay, but God forbid something happens to her. I wouldn't have a clue where to look for half of our assets. That makes me so angry . . ." He then turned toward her and stated, "Each time I bring this up, you dismiss me. That's not fair!"

Career Needs versus Marital Needs

Striking a balance between career needs and marital needs can be difficult. Often a marriage suffers when spouses put their career needs before their marriage. The following observations from a spouse whose husband had separated from her illustrate how difficult it is to keep this balance in our marriages. "I couldn't ignore my business' needs and demands, and I expected him to understand. We fought and fought over the long hours I was keeping until life was no longer any fun . . . If he'll give our marriage a second chance, I plan to make some changes. One thing I will do is pray more and yell less. Another thing I will do is find more time for us."

> STRIKING A BALANCE BETWEEN CAREER NEEDS AND MARITAL NEEDS CAN BE DIFFICULT.

Enjoy, but within Reason

Many couples these days fail to live within their means and purchase whatever they want, when they want, without thinking twice about how their bills will be paid. Sadly, researchers, clergy, and couples therapists are reporting that this pattern is pervasive. No doubt it is important that we enjoy the fruits of our labors, but within reason. When couples fail to live by this principle, serious money issues that trigger arguments and compromise marital satisfaction usually emerge. The high bankruptcy rates illustrate this point. Many couples who file for bankruptcy end up also filing for divorce.

> NO DOUBT IT IS IMPORTANT THAT WE ENJOY THE FRUITS OF OUR LABORS, BUT WITHIN REASON.

Marriage Is a Partnership

Marriage is not a dictatorship; it is a partnership. The following verse in scripture reinforces this observation: "It is not good for man to be alone; I will make him a helper fit for him" (Genesis 2:18). The phrase "a helper fit for him" does not suggest that God created woman to be man's servant. "A helper fit for him" indicates that God created woman to be man's partner who is at once suitable for him and completes him. So how does this apply to a couple's finances?

Whether you have a marriage where one spouse is the provider and the other stays home, or a marriage where both spouses have careers, spouses should seek to cultivate a partnership in all dimensions of their lives—including their finances. In most cases when one spouse assumes a subordinate position and the other a dominant position, this unequal position often compromises the partnership.

Men and Women Have Different Approaches

Gender differences regarding money matters can potentially create problems for couples. That is because men's and women's attitudes regarding money can generally be different. For example, research suggests that men tend to be greater risk takers than women.

Keeping this potential gender difference in mind when you reach couple gridlock related to your money matters can be helpful. In cases when gridlock occurs, it is important for each spouse to avoid becoming entrenched in his or her position. A better option is to ask God for patience, forgiveness, and increased understanding.

Christ's Perspective

Jesus addressed money matters regularly. In fact, He had more to say about this topic than almost any other subject. Within his statements and teachings, He sought to help us understand that a balanced perspective regarding our treasures (money and other assets) can have a profound effect on our well-being and on our relationship with God and our neighbor. For example, He taught, "For where your treasure is, there will your heart be" (Matthew 6:21). Elsewhere He also taught, "For what does it profit a man to gain the whole world and forfeit his life?" (Mark 8:36). In both instances, Jesus was not condemning those who acquire wealth and success. These teachings seek to help us acquire a balanced perspective of

> "FOR WHAT DOES IT PROFIT A MAN TO GAIN THE WHOLE WORLD AND FORFEIT HIS LIFE?" (MARK 8:36)

money and how much it matters. Living a Christ-centered life can help us acquire this perspective. Such a choice is not simply an investment in your financial well-being, but also an investment in your marriage and family.

As a way to bring closure to this chapter, I have decided to end with the following story. I believe this story illustrates how a balanced perspective regarding money matters can enhance our lives or detract from them.

The Investment Banker's Wisdom

An investment banker was standing on a fishing pier in a small coastal village when a small boat with one fisherman docked. Inside the small boat were several large fish. The banker complimented the fisherman on his catch and asked how long it had taken him to catch them.

The fisherman replied, "Only a little while."

The banker then asked why he didn't stay out longer to catch more fish.

The fisherman stated that he had enough fish to support his family's immediate needs.

The banker then asked, "So, what do you do with the rest of your time?'

The fisherman said, "I sleep; fish a little; play with my children; take afternoon naps with my wife, Maria; and each evening I stroll into the village, where I sip wine and play the bouzouki with my friends. I have a full and busy life."

The investment banker scoffed, "I am a Harvard MBA and could help you. You should spend more time fishing, and with the proceeds, buy a bigger boat. With the profits from this bigger boat you could eventually buy several boats and someday own a fleet of fishing boats. Instead of selling your catch to a go-between, you would sell directly to a processor, eventually opening your own cannery. You would control the product, processing, and distribution. You can then leave this small fishing village and move to Athens, or Los Angeles, or New York City, where you will run your expanding enterprise."

The fisherman asked, "But how long will that take?"

"About fifteen to twenty years," replied the banker.

"But what then?" asked the fisherman.

The banker laughed and said, "That's the best part. When the time is right, you would announce an IPO and sell your company stock to the public and become very, very rich."

"Then what?" wondered the fisherman.

"Well, then you would retire. Move to a small coastal fishing village, where you would sleep late, fish a little, play with your kids, take afternoon naps with your wife, and in the evening stroll to the village, where you could sip wine and play the bouzouki with your friends."

Questions for Reflection

1. On a scale of 1 to 10, with 1 representing "we have major financial problems" and 10 representing "we have no problems," how would you rate yourselves?

2. If you scored a 6 or below in the first question, what steps are you going to take to remove the stress that your failed financial practices cause you? List them below.

3. Do you believe that more arguing about finances helps?

4. Which of the strategies found in this chapter could help you? List them.

5. If you are considering a second marriage and you suspect money matters may create some issues and problems, how do you intend to address these issues?

6. If you have already remarried and money matters are a problem, how will you respectfully handle these issues?

RECOMMENDED READING

- *Linking Economic Hardship to Marital Quality and Instability.* Conger, R. D., G. H. Elder, F. O. Lorenz, K. J. Conger, R. L. Simons, L. B. Whitbeck, S. Huck, and J. N. Melby. 1990. Journal of Marriage and Family 52 (3): 643–656.

- *Money Doesn't Buy Happiness, but It Helps: Marital Satisfaction, Psychological Distress, and Demographic Differences between Low- and Middle-Income Clinic Couples.* Dakin, J., and R. Wampler. 2008. American Journal of Family Therapy 356: 300–311.

- *Money and Marriage: The State of Our Unions.* Wilcox, W. B., E. Marquardt, and D. Popenoe. 2009. New York: Institute for American Values.

Resources for Those Experiencing Money Problems

- *Smart Couples Finish Rich: 9 Steps to Creating a Rich Future for You and Your Partner.* Bach, D. 2002. New York: Broadway Books.

- *Debt-Proof Your Marriage: How to Achieve Financial Harmony.* Hunt, M. 2003. Grand Rapids, MI: Fleming H. Revell Publishing.

- *The Total Money Makeover: A Proven Plan for Financial Success.* Ramsey, D. 2009. 3rd ed. Nashville, TN: Thomas Nelson.

HELPFUL WEBSITES

www.SmartMarriages.com

www.daveramsey.com

RECOVERING FROM INFIDELITY: PART I

"Let him who is without sin among you be the first to throw a stone at her."
—John 8:7 (the story of the woman caught in adultery)

What Do I Do If My Spouse Is Cheating on Me?

Dear Father Charles,

I recently found out that my husband has been cheating on me for a few months now. When I confronted him, he denied everything and got really angry. After we argued, he promised not to have any further contact with her. Since he made that promise, he has continued to talk with her. I think I have also found more evidence of some cheating. . . . I have mixed feelings about my marriage, and I don't know what to do. We have three young children. I would like to try to save the marriage for their sake. I am too embarrassed to consult my priest. I wonder if God is punishing me. I hope you can provide some direction.
—E-mail respondent

I am sorry for the heartache and turmoil you are experiencing. Please know that your faith in God can be helpful to you during this very difficult time and that God is not punishing you. In addition, as long as there are no other serious forms of destructive behavior present in your marriage, such as physical abuse, alcohol abuse, chronic gambling, or addictions, I support your desire to save your marriage. Here are a few suggestions that I pray will be helpful as you address the unsettling issues you are facing.

It's Not an Easy Process

As you struggle to try to reclaim your marriage, remember that many couples manage to survive infidelity. Ad-

> MANY COUPLES MANAGE TO SURVIVE INFIDELITY.

mittedly, it is not an easy process, because the trust between spouses has been seriously breached. However, many couples who commit to a recovery process not only survive infidelity but find their marriages strengthened by their efforts to recover from the brokenness caused by the infidelity.

Find a Good Reason to Justify the Effort

It is important for you to find a good reason to justify the effort. This is a vital first step because the recovery process may be one of the hardest tasks you and your spouse will accomplish in your lifetime. Identifying a good reason to enter the recovery process can give you the needed staying power to hang in there when circumstances look bleak and you are second-guessing yourself. In your case, it seems as if the reason for considering the choice to try to save your marriage is for the sake of your three young children. Based on our Church's teachings regarding the well-being of children, coupled with the findings of research, fighting for your marriage for the sake of your children is a compelling and admirable reason that I certainly endorse.

> FIGHTING FOR YOUR MARRIAGE FOR THE SAKE OF YOUR CHILDREN IS A COMPELLING AND ADMIRABLE REASON.

Find a Marriage Therapist

You will need professional help for the recovery process. I encourage you to consider consulting a marriage-friendly therapist in your area who has experience working with marital conflict and infidelity. The following websites should be helpful in finding the professional help you will need: www.marriagefriendlytherapists.com and www.aamft.org. Each site has a therapist locator, which will help you identify skilled therapists in your area. Review the profiles carefully and begin making a list of qualified professionals whose profiles appeal to you.

Get Your Spouse on Board

Once you've identified a few therapists who appear to possess the experience and skills you need, find an opportune time to respectfully broach this subject with your husband to obtain his approval. WARNING: Do not confront, criticize, or attack. Simply approach him with a dispassionate, thoughtful, serious, and prayerful demeanor and tell him that you believe you both have problems that require some professional help. Then ask him if he would be willing to get some professional help with you. At first, he might dismiss your suggestion. If he does, do not become reactive. Simply repeat yourself and give him the space necessary to consider what you've suggested. If he consents to getting help, show him the names of the therapists you have found and suggest that he review their profiles. You might also volunteer to arrange the initial consultation, with the understanding that he agrees with this protocol. Again, as you are attempting to reach some agreement, avoid slipping into an argument. Another argument will simply create more emotional distance between you and exacerbate the issues and problems that exist.

If your spouse refuses to seek outside help, I suggest that you make an appointment and go on your own. Your efforts may eventually lead him to have a change of heart. Keep the door open by periodically inviting him to attend therapy with you. Depending on the circumstances, at this juncture you might concurrently seek legal counsel. This initiative is intended to simply provide you with a better understanding of the family laws in your state regarding legal separation and divorce.

Consult Your Priest

When the time is right—preferably sooner rather than later—consult your priest. I realize this suggestion may evoke some discomfort and embarrassment. However, please remember that priests are not in the habit of judging, and their pastoral counsel and support can be invaluable as you seek healing.

Read a Book

You might also consider reviewing a resource like Shirley Glass' book *Not Just Friends,* or Rona Subotnik and Gloria Harris' book *Surviving Infidelity.* These books and others are available on www.amazon.com. I have often suggested such resources to spouses and couples trying to recover from infidelity, as they help to confirm the normalcy of the emotional pain you experience at any given point in the recovery process and provide valuable information.

Like a Roller Coaster

Keep in mind that the recovery process will at times seem like a roller coaster ride that has no end in sight. However, regardless of how difficult the journey, the pain and distress associated with recovery generally pales by comparison to the emotional scars that divorce leaves on all family members.

A Few Concluding Thoughts

Infidelity does not simply affect the spouses involved. Its debilitating effects, which are well-documented by research, extend far beyond the couple to the children, their extended families, friends, the couple's church family, and many other social networks. The effects of infidelity on children are of the greatest concern. Committing to the emotionally arduous process of recovery is a good and righteous effort that can potentially have a long-lasting positive effect on all concerned, to God's glory and your salvation.

Questions for Reflection

- What do you think about the possibility of a marriage recovering and even thriving after infidelity?

- If your marriage has been impacted by infidelity, what do you think about the possible resources for seeking help? Which ones are most fitting for you and your spouse?

- What do you think about approaching your priest to help support you through the process of recovering from infidelity?

RECOMMENDED READING

- *Not Just Friends: Rebuilding Trust and Recovering Your Sanity after Infidelity.* Glass, S. 2003. New York: Free Press.

- *Adult Children of Parental Infidelity and Their Perspectives of Love, Intimate Relationships, and Marriage.* Koski, M. A. 2001. MS thesis, University of Wisconsin-Stout. Accessed May 9, 2012. http://www2.wwstout.edu/content/lib/thesis/2001/2001koskim.pdf.

- *Genograms.* McGoldrick, M., R. Gerson, and S. Petry. 2008. New York: Norton Company.

- *How Children Are Impacted by Marital Infidelity.* Nogales, A. 2009. Accessed May 9, 2012. http://www.ananogales.com.

- *Surviving Infidelity: Making Decisions, Recovering from the Pain.* Subotnik, R., and G. Harris. 2006. 3rd ed. Avon, MA: Media Books.

WEBSITES

- **Hopeandhealing.us** – Hope & Healing is a Christian-based support ministry devoted entirely to helping couples who have experienced the heartache of adultery. It is led by couples who also have experienced this heartache, are still married, and are committed to being the husbands and wives God intended them to be. Hope & Healing was founded and designed to support, encourage, offer hope, and provide practical strategies for couples willing to grow through this crisis in their marriage.

- **Marriagebuilders.com** – This is a great website, featuring Dr. Willard F. Harley, Jr., which has a whole section devoted to the subject of infidelity and many other subjects on marriage. You will also be introduced to some of the best ways to overcome marital conflicts and some of the quickest ways to restore love. Dr. Harley has saved thousands of marriages from the pain of unresolved conflict and the disaster of divorce. His successful approach to building marriages can help you build yours. There's even a discussion forum that you can use to ask questions.

RECOVERING FROM INFIDELITY: PART II

"Trust in the Lord with all your heart, and do not rely on your insight. In all your ways acknowledge Him, and He will make straight your paths." — *Proverbs 3:5–6*

What Does Recovery Involve?

Infidelity is a serious breach of trust in a marriage, although many couples can and do recover. If a couple chooses and engages in the path of recovery, the process is painful and difficult, but the potential outcome is a dynamic, vibrant, and life-giving marriage. Some parts of the path may be more difficult than others, and you might get stuck along the way for a while. However, there is no getting around it. Both you and your spouse must walk this path to get to the other side.

One spouse whose husband was unfaithful said, "Trying to regain what I lost when I discovered that my husband was cheating on me on business trips was one of the hardest challenges I ever faced. In retrospect, I'm happy I didn't seek a divorce. I was able to hang in there to determine if there was any future for us. Two years later, the effort was worth it. We are closer today to one another than we ever have been. Is therapy for everyone when one spouse has been unfaithful? I doubt it, but it was for me. For the sake of our children and family, before considering divorce I needed to know if we could repair the damage my husband's affair caused."

This quote validates two important findings of research on infidelity:

- Some couples successfully recover from an affair (Glass 2003; Sobotnik and Harris 2006).
- The hard work and commitment to the recovery process after an affair sometimes lead to an increased level of intimacy and connection between husband and wife that did not exist before the affair (Glass 2003; Sobotnik and Harris 2006).

What follows is a brief description of a recovery process that therapists typically use to help couples recover from infidelity. However, I would not recommend that couples try to work through these steps alone. This information is offered to illustrate the typical healing steps that therapists and couples follow toward recovery. If, once you enter into therapy, you find that the process does not resemble what is suggested in this chapter and that, after six to eight sessions, the process is not helping, you should consider finding another therapist.

Stage One: Zero Contact

In order for the recovery process to begin, both spouses must commit to a minimum of six months of marriage work. This minimum time commitment acknowledges the severity of the breach caused by the infidelity and the difficult work that the recovery process will require.

> IN ORDER FOR THE RECOVERY PROCESS TO BEGIN, BOTH SPOUSES MUST COMMIT TO A MINIMUM OF SIX MONTHS OF MARRIAGE WORK.

Concurrent with a six-month commitment, the offending spouse needs to terminate any and all contact with his or her partner in the affair. If the offending spouse is continuing to meet with his or her affair partner and is unwilling to end the affair, this is usually an indication that the offending spouse is not ready to do the difficult work that is required. I will then either provide a referral or suggest other options.

When the offending spouse has either ended the affair or expresses a desire to work toward zero contact, I will work with the couple so long as (1) the spouse who has been victimized is committed to the process I outline, and (2) the offender offers assurances that he or she has either ended the affair or intends to end it within a reasonable time frame—usually a few days—and is committed to working on repairing the damage he or she has caused.

Stage Two: Information and Questions

Once both spouses are reasonably certain that zero contact has been achieved, a period of information and questions unfolds. This stage is guided by the spouse who has been victimized, and it usually creates a great deal of discomfort for the unfaithful spouse. During this stage, I try to hold the couple in a safe place, while granting the victim the latitude to ask as many questions as he or she needs to ask. This is a necessary part of the recovery process, as it permits the victim the space to carefully understand what happened and why it happened, and to determine if he or she sees any future for the relationship. As the unfaithful spouse begins to "come clean" about his or her infidelity, the rebuilding of trust may also begin to occur.

Stage Three: Remorse and Compassion

As the second stage unfolds and the offending spouse begins to realize the level of damage, pain, and hurt caused by the infidelity, the hope is that the unfaithful partner will begin to feel remorse for his or her actions. Because regret and remorse generally evoke human compassion, hopefully the offended spouse will slowly begin to feel some compassion for the offending spouse. If this dynamic occurs, the therapy will slowly move to the next stage.

Stage Four: Rebuilding Trust

Remorse and compassion slowly guide the couple to a process of trust building. The spouse who has been victimized begins to let go of his or her concerns and questions and to slowly trust again. During this juncture, new rules and new boundaries that feel comfortable to both spouses—especially the offended spouse—are established. Then the spouses begin to engage in more talk that alludes to a life together rather than apart. These exchanges stand in stark contrast to

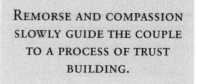

REMORSE AND COMPASSION SLOWLY GUIDE THE COUPLE TO A PROCESS OF TRUST BUILDING.

the couple's initial conversations, which focused on individual plans, dreams, and aspirations. As trust building continues, spouses commonly make statements like: "If he's late and fails to call home, my whole world doesn't begin to come crashing down around me. I'm upset, but not overwhelmed. I know that things happen, so I can wait until he gets home to hear what he has to say. . . . I guess this means I trust him more, but I still need some verbal assurances that his failure to call home wasn't just him taking me for granted."

Stage Five: Forgiveness

Genuine forgiveness begins to emerge when: the offending spouse understands and communicates with sincere remorse the severity of what he or she did and how this behavior affected his or her spouse, marriage, and family; and the offending spouse can offer sincere assurances that such behavior will never happen again. These actions do not presuppose that the offended spouse will immediately accept the apology. In fact, usually the offending spouse must offer multiple apologies before the offended spouse will accept the apology. Once the offended spouse is able to accept the apology, the couple is able to move on from the debilitating effects of the affair toward a future together.

Concluding Thoughts

The nature of infidelity is sufficiently serious to be listed among the few reasons the Orthodox Church will grant an ecclesiastical divorce. In some cases when infidelity occurs—especially repeated patterns of infidelity—some couples cannot recover from the serious breach caused by the actions of the offending spouse. In these instances, the marriage is dead, and reconciliation is impossible.

Despite the devastating effects of infidelity on marriages, research findings indicate that a significant percentage of marriages can be saved. This chapter has sought to illustrate a process that assists couples in repairing the serious breach caused by infidelity. If both partners are willing to do what it takes to repair the breach, with the grace of God, many couples can successfully recover.

Questions for Reflection

• If infidelity is an issue in your marriage, where are you and your spouse located in regard to your desire to reclaim your marriage and recover from the infidelity? Using a scale of 1 to 10 to help answer this question might be helpful.

• Which steps do you think may be the most difficult for you? For your spouse?

• Where is God in each of your lives and in your life as a couple, especially in regard to the issue of infidelity?

RECOMMENDED READING

• ***Not Just Friends: Rebuilding Trust and Recovering Your Sanity after Infidelity.*** Glass, S. 2003. New York: Free Press.

• ***Surviving Infidelity: Making Decisions, Recovering from the Pain.*** Subotnik, R., and G. Harris. 2006. 3rd ed. Avon, MA: Media Books.

WEBSITES

• **Hopeandhealing.us** – Hope & Healing is a Christian-based support ministry devoted entirely to helping couples who have experienced the heartache of adultery. It is led by couples who also have experienced this heartache, are still married, and are committed to being the husbands and wives God intended them to be. Hope & Healing was founded and designed to support, encourage, offer hope, and provide practical strategies for couples willing to grow through this crisis in their marriage.

• **Marriagebuilders.com** – This is a great website, featuring Dr. Willard F. Harley, Jr., which has a whole section devoted to the subject of infidelity and many other subjects on marriage. You will also be introduced to some of the best ways to overcome marital conflicts and some of the quickest ways to restore love. Dr. Harley has saved thousands of marriages from the pain of unresolved conflict and the disaster of divorce. His successful approach to building marriages can help you build yours. There's even a discussion forum that you can use to ask questions.

DOMESTIC VIOLENCE
AND MARRIAGE

"My grace is sufficient for you, for My power is made perfect in weakness."
–2 Corinthians 12:9

COAUTHORED BY KERRY PAPPAS, MA, LMFT

Introduction

The most recent survey from the Center for Disease Control (CDC 2010) found that one in four women and one in seven men are victims of serious physical abuse by an "intimate partner" (www.cdc.gov/ Violence Prevention). Many other detailed statistics are available. Nev-

> ONE IN FOUR WOMEN AND ONE IN SEVEN MEN ARE VICTIMS OF SERIOUS PHYSICAL ABUSE BY AN "INTIMATE PARTNER."

ertheless, all of the data confirm that the most serious physical and sexual abuse is inflicted on women. The Greek Orthodox community is not immune to this problem (Geanacopoulos 1999).

For the purpose of this chapter, it is helpful for the reader to keep in mind the following:

• The term "intimate partner abuse" will be used to refer to the abuse of both men and women in intimate relationships.

• Given the contemporary reality that both men and women abuse their spouses, when Saint John Chrysostom is quoted using the language of wife abuse, the reader should broaden the term to include all intimate partner abuse.

• Abuse takes on many forms: physical, emotional, verbal, sexual, economic, and isolation. Thus, the incidence of abuse is far greater than the cases of physical and sexual abuse that are reported.

• The incidence of physical and/or sexual abuse is likely greater than what is reported because many who are abused fear the possible repercussions of reporting the abuse.

The Effects of Abuse

Abuse has serious, noxious consequences on individual, couple, and family well-being. For the sake of brevity, only the most common and serious consequences will be reviewed.

Victims of physical abuse sustain physical injuries that range from life-threatening conditions to minor injuries, whereas victims of physical and/or other forms of abuse often exhibit chronic health problems, stress, depression, anxiety, panic, increased incidence of suicide, and financial difficulties (Barnett 2001; Jones and Horan 1997, Vitanza et al. 1995).

After a couple is married, all forms of abuse, particularly physical, are serious deterrents to the marriage remaining intact, thus contributing to the cycle of broken marriages (Fettig, McLanahan, and Garfinkel 2002).

Children who witness abuse are more likely to experience socioemotional and developmental difficulties (Christopoulos et al. 1987; Dodd 2009) and are at much greater risk for exercising violent behavior as adults, thus perpetuating the cycle of physical abuse in future generations [www.ncadv.org/files/DomesticVio lenceFactSheet(National).pdf].

The Church's Understanding of Marriage

We live in a postmodern, secular age. As such, it is not uncommon for members of our society to view marriage as a human construction that has evolved through social consensus, or to place a positive value on marriage so long as it serves to enhance emotional, social, economic, and psychological well-being. Greek Orthodox Christians are no exception. Most espouse perspectives of marriage that are profoundly influenced by dominant American values rather than Church teachings. One Greek Orthodox man's statements illustrate this point.

> THE CHURCH HAS ALWAYS LIFTED MARRIAGE OUT OF A PRAGMATIC, MUNDANE, AND SECULAR CONTEXT AND CONTEXTUALIZED IT WITHIN THE LIFE IN CHRIST.

While pondering relational issues with his fiancée two months before their wedding, he stated, "People get married because they are looking for a soul mate—someone who's going to meet some of your basic needs. . . . You know, like, to listen to you, support you, build a family with you." When asked what his faith background teaches about marriage, he said, "To be honest with you, I really don't know what the Church would have to say about this."

The Church has always lifted marriage out of a pragmatic, mundane, and secular context and contextualized it within the life in Christ. This understanding of marriage is clearly reflected in the Old Testament and in the teachings of Jesus Christ, Saint Paul, other Church fathers and mothers, and theologians throughout the centuries. For the Church, marriage is not predicated on what is deemed socially, politically, legally, economically, or philosophically correct. Rather, marriage is entirely dependent on certain divinely revealed truths that have emerged as God has manifested Himself to humankind, beginning with our ancestors, Adam and Eve. Among these divine truths, the following assertions and presuppositions are of central importance:

- In marriage, the spiritual—as well as physical, emotional, economic, and social—needs of each spouse are taken into account, as evidenced in the service of the sacrament of marriage.

- Marriage is an eternal gift and bond from God, not a contract between two persons who vow to commit themselves to each other until "death do us [them] part" (Meyendorff 1975).

- Marriage is a divinely revealed way of existence, not a human construction that has evolved through social consensus (Zion 1992).

- The relationship of the husband and wife is understood to be an image of the relationship of Christ and the Church (Meyendorff 1975; Stylianopoulos 1977; Zion 1992).

- Marriage is a sacrament, "the sacrament of love" (Evdokimov 1985, 105), and, as such, it is the sacred place in which husband and wife learn to love.

- In marriage, husband and wife journey together, toward realizing their full humanity in Christ and participating in God's Kingdom. In the words of Father John Meyendorff, marriage "is a unique union of two beings in love, two beings who can transcend their own humanity and thus be united not only 'with each other,' but also 'in Christ'" (Meyendorff 1975, 17).

- The ultimate purpose of marriage is the salvation of both spouses (Meyendorff 1975; Stylianopoulos 1977; Zion 1992).

The Incongruity of Marriage and Abuse

Given the Church's understanding of marriage, it is clear that spousal abuse has no place in this sacred institution because it undermines a couple's efforts to cultivate a Christian marriage.

Saint John Chrysostom provides the following insights and counsel to husbands:

> [Christ] offered Himself up for [the Church,] who turned her back on Him and hated Him. In the same way . . . as He accomplished this not with threats, or terror, or anything else like that, but through His untiring love; so also you should behave toward your wife. Even if you see her belittling you, or despising and mocking you, still you will be able to subject her to yourself, through affection, kindness, and your great regard for her. There is no influence more powerful than the bond of love, especially for husband and wife. . . . But one's partner for life, the mother of one's children, the source of one's every joy, should never be fettered with fear and threats, but with love and patience. What kind of marriage can there be when the wife is afraid of her husband? What sort of satisfaction could a husband have, if he lives with his wife as if she were a slave, and not a woman by her own free will? (Chrysostom 1986, 46–47)

This quotation by Saint John Chrysostom reveals and implies a number of important observations about spousal abuse:

- Just as Christ loves the Church, husbands are exhorted to exercise patience and self-sacrifice in loving their wives; this leaves no excuse for violence, abuse, or controlling behavior.

- God created humans to be free. Thus, husbands are called to respect their wives' free will, just as God respects the freedom of all humans.

> "THERE IS NO INFLUENCE MORE POWERFUL THAN THE BOND OF LOVE, ESPECIALLY FOR HUSBAND AND WIFE."
> (SAINT JOHN CHRYSOSTOM)

- When husbands choose abusive, controlling behavior in responding to their wives, they compromise the inherent God-given benefits that husbands and wives can potentially experience in a Christian marriage.

- In reminding husbands of their children, Saint John Chrysostom suggests the negative effects of abuse on children and the family's spiritual well-being.

- Husbands are called to repent and to turn to God's life-transforming grace to stop abusive behaviors.

For Those in Abusive Relationships

- Have you minimized your partner's abusive behavior with thoughts like the following? "It's my fault. I caused him [her] to lose his temper." "He [she] didn't mean it; he [she] still loves me." "He [she] really doesn't mean to hurt me." "He [she] is under a lot of pressure." "He [she] is doing the best he [she] can do." These are red flags that suggest you need help.

- You are not responsible for your spouse's abusive behavior. He or she is responsible for it.

- Do fear, anxiety, helplessness, confusion, and shame overwhelm you when you consider reaching out for help? Do these feelings render you incapable of finding the help you need? These are red flags that suggest you need help.

- Trust your feelings; if you feel unsafe, you are unsafe.

- God is not punishing you for anything you have done wrong; you do not deserve to be abused!

- Have a clear plan for leaving the house and going to a safe place.

- Seek the help of your priest, family members, friends, and/or a professional counselor.

- If you have children, make sure they are protected. Those who abuse their spouses are more likely to also abuse their children.

> ABUSIVE BEHAVIOR HARMS THE SPIRITUAL, EMOTIONAL, RELATIONAL, AND MENTAL WELL-BEING OF INDIVIDUALS, COUPLES, AND FAMILIES AND CLEARLY VIOLATES THE CHURCH'S UNDERSTANDING OF THE NATURE AND PURPOSE OF MARRIAGE.

- Make sure you have some money put away in case you need to leave the house suddenly.

- Maintain easy access to important legal documents.

These "guidelines" are based on standard treatment protocols that are accepted by psychotherapists who work with victims of domestic violence. As such, victims of domestic violence, clergy, psychotherapists, and concerned family members should view them as helpful guidelines and not as a replacement for professional help. Professionals with special training and experience treating domestic violence should be consulted for support, coaching, and additional insights.

Additionally, many online resources, telephone hotlines, and books are available to those in abusive relationships. A few of these resources are listed at the end of this chapter.

Conclusion

The Church's understanding of the nature of the marriage relationship, coupled with the findings of social science research, points to the following conclusions regarding spousal abuse: Abusive behavior harms the spiritual, emotional, relational, and mental well-being of individuals, couples, and families and clearly violates the Church's understanding of the nature and purpose of marriage.

Questions for Reflection

- What do you understand physical abuse to be?

- What do you understand emotional and verbal abuse to be?

- Do you believe that abuse in any form is to be tolerated or not? If some abuse is to be tolerated, where do you draw the line?

- If you are in an abusive relationship, how is the relationship understood in relation to the will of God and in the Church's understanding of marriage?

- If you abuse or are the victim of abuse, what steps have you taken to address the abuse, and what steps do you still need to take? When and where will you go for help?

REFERENCES ON MARRIAGE AND THE EFFECTS OF ABUSE

- *Why Battered Women Do Not Leave, Part 2: External Inhibiting Factors—Social Support and Internal Inhibiting Factors.* Trauma, Violence, and Abuse 2 (1): 3–35. Barnett, O. 2001.

- *Children of Abused Women: Adjustment at Time of Shelter Residence.* Journal of Marriage and Family 49 (3): 611–619. Christopoulos, C., D. A. Cohn, D. S. Shaw, S. Joyce, J. Sullivan-Hanson, S. P. Kraft, and R. Emery. 1987.

- *On Marriage and Family Life.* Chrysostom, St. John. 1986. Translated by C. P. Roth. Crestwood, NY: St. Vladimir's Seminary Press.

- *Therapeutic Group Work with Young Children and Mothers Who Have Experienced Domestic Abuse.* Educational Psychology in Practice 25 (1): 21–36. Dodd, Lynda Warren. 2009.

- *The Sacrament of Love.* Evdokimov, Paul. 1985. Crestwood, NY: St. Vladimir's Seminary Press.

- *Child Support Enforcement and Domestic Violence among Non-cohabitating Couples.* Working paper #02-17-FF. Fretig, A., S. McLanaham, and I. Garfinkel. 2002. Center for Research on Child Wellbeing, Princeton University.

- *Domestic Violence: A Training Manual for the Greek Orthodox Community.* Geanacopoulos, P. 1999. New York: Greek Orthodox Archdiocese of America.

- *The American College of Obstetricians and Gynecologists: A Decade of Responding to Violence against Women.* International Journal of Gynecology and Obstetrics 58 (1): 43–50. Jones, F. R., and D. L. Horan. 1997.

- *Marriage: An Orthodox Perspective.* Meyendorff, John. 1975. Crestwood, NY: St. Vladimir's Seminary Press.

- *Distress and Symptoms of Posttraumatic Stress Disorder in Abused Women.* Violence and Victims 10 (1): 23–34. Vitanza, S., L. C. Vogel, and L. L. Marshall. 1995.

- *Eros and Transformation: Sexuality and Marriage from an Eastern Orthodox Perspective.* Zion, W. B. 1992. New York: University Press of America.

RESOURCES FOR THOSE IN ABUSIVE RELATIONSHIPS

Books

- *Getting Free: You Can End Abuse and Take Back Your Life.* NiCarthy, G. 1997. Seattle: Seal Press.

- *You Don't Have to Take It Anymore.* Stosny, Steven. 2005. New York: Free Press.

Domestic Violence Resources

- National Domestic Violence Hotline: 800-799-SAFE (7233)

- Christian Coalition Against Domestic Abuse: www.ccada.org

WEBSITES

www.cdc.gov/violenceprevention

www.joyfulheartfoundation.org

www.safehorizon.org

www.womenthrive.org

No More Secrets: Sexual Addictions And Compulsions

"All things are lawful for me, but not all things are helpful. All things are lawful for me, but I will not be enslaved by anything."
–1 Corinthians 6:12

(This chapter addresses sexual addiction and compulsion. Despite this focus, most of the information that follows also relates to those who use pornography or engage in sex blogs, sex chat rooms, sadomasochism role- playing, and other similar activities. If you engage in these behaviors or other similar cyber and/or sexual activities, please consider reviewing the information that follows. It could have a marked, positive impact on you and your marriage.)

Franklin calls a therapist and says, "I have some bad habits I need help with." When the therapist asks him to elaborate, silence ensues. The therapist is patient and waits. Franklin finally states, "My wife discovered I'm viewing porn online. She's done a thorough search of the sites I had bookmarked—we've sanitized the computer. Now she's telling me I have to find some help, and if I don't, we're done. I want to save my marriage. Can you help?"

Kosta calls a therapist. He is a bank president who says he is struggling with anxiety and can't sleep. As therapy progresses, a bank audit reveals that he has been embezzling funds for women with whom he's had sexual liaisons on the Internet.

Irene, a doctor, has been in therapy for six months. Prior to beginning therapy, she was meeting violent men online anonymously for "rough" sex. During one encounter she was beaten and left for dead, and she nearly died. Upon discovering the secret life his wife was leading, her husband considered filing for divorce but instead opted to enter into treatment with her. In treatment she's learned that her stepfather's abusive treatment affected her arousal patterns and her proclivity to engage in compulsive behavior—behavior and choices that nearly killed her.

How Common Is Sex Addiction?

Franklin, Kosta, and Irene are not isolated cases. Although it is difficult to de-termine how many people struggle with sexual addictions and compulsions, estimates suggest that approximately 4.5% of the population (12 million people) may grapple with sexual addiction and compulsions in the United States (Carnes 2001). Moreover, with the advent of the Internet and the endless number of sites available, there is good reason to suggest this disorder may be on the rise.

> ESTIMATES SUGGEST THAT APPROXIMATELY 4.5% OF THE POPULATION (12 MILLION PEOPLE) MAY GRAPPLE WITH SEXUAL ADDICTION AND COMPULSIONS IN THE UNITED STATES.

Caught in the Grip

Sexual addiction is a serious problem. Persons caught in the grip of this disorder cannot easily break free without competent professional help. Persistent escalating patterns and distorted thoughts tend to overwhelm them and pull them into unwanted behavior patterns. Much like Franklin, Kosta, and Irene, when addicts fail to seek treatment, the behaviors increase and eventually create negative consequences for them and their closest relationships (Carnes 2001). Regardless of the escalating costs, sex addicts will pursue the "high" and/or "anesthetic" they receive from engaging in certain aberrant sexual behaviors that feed their addiction and compulsions. Because shame is part and parcel of the behaviors they engage in, sex addicts generally do not seek help until something happens that forces them to get help.

In short, sex addicts are very much like other addicts. They are commonly victims of childhood abuse and neglect, and their potentially destructive feelings and compulsive behaviors are often the result of mismanaged fear of intimacy, anger, and resentment, rooted in the negative view of sex espoused by their family of origin (Carnes 2001). These early experiences provide a foundation from which later sexual acting out manifests itself.

Red Flags

If you've been struggling with inappropriate sexual compulsions and/or behaviors but you believe that these behaviors suggest you simply have an overactive libido, I urge you to review the following questions. The reality is that the behaviors you are struggling with will likely have a negative impact on your well-being, your marriage, and your family.

- Are you engaged in persistent, self-destructive behavior?
- Do you engage in persistent thoughts and fantasies as a primary coping strategy to help you relieve tension and anxiety?

- Have you found yourself engaging in increased amounts of unwanted sexual behaviors because previous levels of sexual activity are no longer sufficient?
- Are you expending an inordinate amount of time obtaining sex, being sexual, or recovering from sexual experiences?
- Are you ashamed of any of your persistent sexual activities?
- Do any of your sexual activities negatively affect your social/recreational life or your job performance?

If you answered "yes" to three or more of these questions, you probably have a serious problem with sex and should seek competent professional help and spiritual counseling. Professionals with experience in sexual addictions and compulsions can assess and confirm whether you have a problem that requires treatment.

Seeking Help

When seeking a therapist, I would encourage you to find someone who treats the disorder from both an individual mental health perspective and a systems perspective. Therapists who take this dual approach use a treatment protocol that addresses sexual addiction at the individual level. However, they believe that persons are also embedded within families and that their problems have a negative impact on their marriages, families, and children. Also, if I were looking for a therapist, I would look for someone who is comfortable with 12-step programs. Research suggests that addicts, their spouses, and other significant family members do better with ongoing support. For more information about these programs, consult the resources at the end of this article. And finally, whomever you select should have advanced training and experience treating sexual addiction and compulsion issues. One simple way to determine if a therapist has sufficient expertise is to review his or her online profile and/or by simply asking the therapist during your initial phone inquiry.

Help for the Marriage

Sooner or later, a spouse discovers most of the secrets of his or her sex-addicted partner. Such discoveries seriously compromise intimacy and trust and may ultimately challenge the viability of a marriage. However, many couples survive this challenge, and, through treatment, they grow closer to one another. With the help of a

> SOONER OR LATER, A SPOUSE DISCOVERS MOST OF THE SECRETS OF HIS OR HER SEX-ADDICTED PARTNER.

therapist, these couples adopt the following strategies (Carnes 1999). Please note that these strategies, along with the remaining information in this chapter, are offered to provide you with a basic, appropriate framework to help you find a therapist; they are not to be used without competent professional help.

- The addict makes his or her recovery a first priority.
- Both spouses choose to connect with a 12-step program.
- Many couples go through extensive couples counseling to identify patterns of behavior that do not work.
- Both spouses accept that the recovery process is a challenging, evolving journey.
- Both spouses educate themselves.
- Both spouses are willing to grow religiously and spiritually.
- Both spouses have a high commitment to saving the marriage and a strong respect for one another.

Beyond these general steps, a good treatment plan will include the following additional steps to facilitate the restoration of relational trust and forgiveness (Carnes 1999).

The Offending Partner

The offending partner must begin by offering his or her spouse an apology. The following steps are usually part and parcel of the treatment process that focuses on facilitating the "oneness" of marriage at the individual and couple levels. The offending spouse must understand how his or her behaviors have hurt his or her spouse.

- He or she must feel the pain and injury his or her behavior caused his or her partner.
- He or she must learn how the behaviors developed and how they can be effectively managed.
- He or she must develop an action plan that will help him or her avoid the hurtful behavior.
- He or she must share the plan with his or her partner and follow through with it.
- He or she must offer a sincere apology.
- He or she must ask for an opportunity to restore trust.

The Betrayed Spouse

The betrayed spouse must understand the injustices his or her partner's behavior inflicted upon him or her.

- He or she must seek to work through feelings of anger and resentment.
- He or she must learn the "red flags" and draw healthy boundaries that are self-protective.
- He or she must make a shift from judging his or her partner to judging the behavior.
- He or she must discern his or her hurtful behaviors in the relationship.
- He or she must stop punishing the other person and/or stop controlling his or her partner.
- He or she must intentionally choose to adopt interactions that facilitate relational intimacy.

How Can Life in Christ Help?

At minimum, healthy, holy sex is considered a gift from God: It meets the emotional and physical needs of each spouse, helps facilitate marital oneness, and positively contributes to each person's struggle toward salvation. Conversely, the aberrant behaviors that sex addicts engage in are inherently ego-centered, self-destructive, other-destructive, and sinful. Such behaviors frustrate a person's relationship with God and seriously undermine a person's relationship with his or her spouse, children, and significant others. Because a sex addict's behaviors are ego-centered and skewed toward self-gratification, such behaviors are sinful because they fall short of God's will (Zion 1992). Moreover, until the sex addict admits his or her "powerlessness" over these destructive behaviors, and until he or she repents and surrenders his or her life to God, he or she will remain distanced from God's life-changing, healing grace. That stated, together with competent professional help, the Church would maintain that sex addicts can greatly benefit from living a life in Christ.

> HEALTHY, HOLY SEX IS CONSIDERED A GIFT FROM GOD: IT MEETS THE EMOTIONAL AND PHYSICAL NEEDS OF EACH SPOUSE, HELPS FACILITATE MARITAL ONENESS, AND POSITIVELY CONTRIBUTES TO EACH PERSON'S STRUGGLE TOWARD SALVATION.

To be more specific, through an effort to live out a life in Christ, the sex addict's life is transformed. The person no longer lives an ego-centered existence that is dominated by the demons from the past and toxic urges and compulsions that fail to assuage his or her anger, shame, and guilt. Further, as the person embraces the Church's liturgical calendar and its sacramental life, studies Holy Scripture, and fellowships with others who are on a similar journey toward salvation, the person is freed from the chains and shackles of sex addiction. Instead, God's life-changing grace helps to transform him or her into the person he or she was created to be.

At a couple and family level, as God's life-transforming, healing grace blesses the addict's life, the healing and change have a qualitatively positive impact on his or her marriage and family. The addict's addictive behaviors no longer undermine oneness. Christ-centered virtues and the gifts of the Holy Spirit (Galatians 5:22) facilitate oneness and a couple's efforts to struggle toward salvation (Mamalakis and Joanides 2010).

Conclusion

Sexual addictions and compulsions undermine a person's spiritual, psychological, emotional, and physical well-being. At the same time, a sex addict's behaviors have a negative impact on marital satisfaction, oneness, and family stability. If left unchecked, addictive behaviors have the potential to destroy lives, marriages, and families. Fortunately, help is available for a sex addict to manage destructive sexual addictions and compulsions. Taking the first step toward corrective measures can make all the difference between being held hostage and being emancipated from the devastating effects of sexual addiction.

A Final Word for the Casual Participant

The focus of this chapter is on sexual addictions. What about those who engage in the casual use of offline and online pornography, sex blogs, sex chat rooms, sadomasochism role-playing, and other similar behaviors? What can be said about these types of activities?

First, with the advent of the Internet, participation in these activities is easier than ever. In fact, since 2003, sex has been the number one product on the Internet (Carnes and Carnes 2010). So, if you are engaged in cybersex but do not consider yourself a sex addict, how does such activity hinder your efforts to cultivate a Christ-like marital lifestyle?

From the Church's perspective, married persons are called to cultivate oneness. However, when we engage in cybersex like the people in the cases described above, such activity ultimately undermines a spouse's efforts to connect and cultivate oneness for the following reasons:

- Cybersex is a misuse of our free will.
- It isolates us from our partner.
- It is ego-centered and seeks self-gratification.
- It is devoid of the love giving and love receiving that characterize a Christ-centered understanding of sex.
- It frustrates a spouse's efforts to connect and cultivate oneness while concurrently doing damage to a person's well-being.

As a result, the Church counsels its faithful to avoid engaging in cybersex. Moreover, if you have been participating in cybersex, please consider the potentially negative effects it can have on your marriage and make a concerted effort to stop. Turning to God on your own and confessing your sins, and/or requesting the sacrament of confession, can help to purge the residual negative effects of cybersex. Taking a proactive approach will bless you, your marriage, and your family.

Questions for Reflection

- If you or your spouse is engaging in questionable sexual practices, what have you done to address the issue?

- What was the attitude toward sex in the home in which you were raised?

- What are the some of the harmful effects of sex addictions on marriage and family life?

- What is your personal attitude toward casual cybersex?

RECOMMENDED READING

- **Out of the Shadows: Understanding Sexual Addiction.** Carnes, P. 2001. 3rd ed. Center City, MN: Hazelden.

- **Open Hearts: Renewing Relationships with Recovery, Romance and Reality.** Carnes, P., D. Laaser, and M. Laaser. 1999. Wickenbury, AZ: Gentle Path Press.

- **The Journey of Marriage in the Orthodox Church.** Mamalakis, P., and C. Joanides. 2010. New York: Greek Orthodox Archdiocese.

- **Eros and Transformation: Sexuality and Marriage from an Eastern Orthodox Perspective.** Zion, W. B. 1992. Lanham: University Press of America.

ONLINE RESOURCES

Sex Addicts Anonymous (SAA): www.sexaa.org

Sexaholics Anonymous (SA): www.sa.org

RECOVERING FROM DIVORCE

"But He knows the way that I take; when He has tried me, I shall come forth as gold." –Job 23:10

Over the past thirty years, 30 to 50% of marriages in the United States have ended in divorce (Dafoe Whitehead and Popenoe 2006). These statistics do not begin to tell the entire story. In the wake of these staggeringly high statistics is a trail of pain and suffering that has negatively impacted hundreds of thousands of souls.

This chapter has been written for those who have suffered a divorce. However, the objective is not to evoke more pain, guilt, and shame. People who have experienced the process of divorce, as our Lord knows, have suffered enough. In keeping with the Church's compassionate, redemptive, and restorative message of hope, the information that follows is intended to provide encouragement, guidance, and assistance to those seeking to recover from the painful process of divorce, so that you might "come forth as gold."

The Orthodox Church's View of Divorce

The Orthodox Church does not promote divorce. It maintains that marriage is not simply a relationship we enter "until death do us part," and further asserts that love relationships transcend death. Spouses continue to maintain a relationship with one another even after death, although the relationship will be qualitatively different. Nevertheless, it endures.

> THE ORTHODOX CHURCH DOES NOT PROMOTE DIVORCE. . . . DESPITE THE STRONG STANCE ON THE ETERNAL NATURE OF MARRIAGE, THE CHURCH ACKNOWLEDGES THAT SOME MARRIAGES CEASE TO BE VIABLE PLACES IN WHICH THOSE INVOLVED CAN "WORK OUT [THEIR] SALVATION IN FEAR AND TREMBLING."
> (PHILIPPIANS 2:12)

Despite its strong stance on the eternal nature of marriage, the Church acknowledges that some marriages cease to be viable places in which those involved can "work out [their] salvation in fear and trembling" (Philippians 2:12). With deep sadness, the Church acknowledges the fact that some marriages die, and maintains that broken and seriously dysfunctional relationships are destructive to the well-being of the spouses and children involved. In these cases, the Church permits its faithful to exit an inherently destructive situation.

The Painful Path toward Divorce

"Divorces don't simply happen. It's not as though people are married one day and they decide to divorce the next day. It's a long, difficult process." An e-mail correspondent shared these words with me. The truth is that divorce is a "difficult process."

Thanks to some valid and reliable research, today we know that divorces are preceded by a lengthy, painful, and predictable period of conflict that places spouses on a very slippery slope toward marital meltdown and divorce (Gottman 1994; Sprenkle 2012). During this process, negativity in the form of criticism, contempt, defensiveness, and stonewalling begins to slowly saturate the exchanges between husband and wife. These toxic interactions slowly poison the ecosystem of a marriage, and negativity undermines mutual trust, understanding, friendship, and love.

Many spouses who get caught on this slippery slope admit to beginning marriage as "soul mates." In time, they feel more like roommates, and eventually end up feeling like cell mates. During a particularly emotional therapy session, an excerpt from one divorced person's remarks describes some of the reasons why marriages fail. "I really wanted it to work, but I simply couldn't live with the same unresolved disagreements. Our arguments resembled a broken record. . . . The finger-pointing and unfair accusations and endless arguing proved to make us both absolutely miserable. In the end, it was just too hard to be together. The pain needed to end. Divorce seemed like the only way out."

After months or even years of seemingly negative interactions or other unresolvable issues that lead to a marital meltdown, one or both spouses is compelled to seek legal counsel, landing the couple in one of our nation's crowded divorce courts. By the time the civil divorce is finalized, the spouses are often emotionally, spiritually, and financially depleted. If children are involved, parents will often remain conflicted for years. It is no wonder that the Holmes and Rahe stress scale, a respected psychometric instrument, ranks divorce as the second most significant stressor affecting adult health and well-being, behind the death of a spouse.

Does God Still Love Me?

If you are suffering or have suffered through the divorce process, you have likely experienced a myriad of mixed feelings ranging from exhilaration and hopefulness to crippling forms of anger, resentment, sadness, guilt, and shame. Experiencing these feelings is a common and normal part of the process (Burns and Whiteman 1998).

One e-mail respondent observed, "In my head I know I was doing the right thing, but in my heart it was harder to accept what happened. Lately I've felt considerable amounts of guilt and shame, often questioning if I am lovable, and even if God still considers me worthy of His love. In my heart I know He does, but in some of my lowest moments, when feelings of guilt and shame overwhelm me, I question everything."

Another e-mail respondent described his feelings this way: "Some days I'm so angry with her for breaking up the family. I'm suffering, and our children are suffering, and I don't think she cares. She's off having a grand old time with her new boyfriend. . . . All this makes me feel like God is somehow punishing me for something."

Divorce has a way of making people question everything about their lives. Regaining perspective; a healthy, holy love of self; and a deeper awareness of God's undying love are crucial to recovering from divorce. Authentic recovery usually includes most of the following "spiritual steps." These steps involve a slow, deliberate process toward recovery. As difficult as these steps may be, they bring healing and a broader, healthier, holier perspective.

- Step toward God and seek to reconnect with Him, however inadequate your efforts.
- When taking the first step, identify and acknowledge your sins rather than your partner's sins.
- Confess your sins.
- Understand and seek repentance.
- Receive and accept God's mercy, forgiveness, and unconditional love.

When taking these steps, most people require some help. As a result, you might consider participating in a divorce support group that has a decidedly Christian orientation. Many groups are available online and, in all likelihood, in your local community. Two online sites that are particularly good sources of information are:
www.divorcecare.com
www.smartmarriages.com

Together with a support group, an optimal approach would also involve your pastor's support and guidance. If your pastor does not provide this type of spiritual counseling, then consider a professional couples counselor who has a Christian orientation and/or is comfortable working with religious populations.

In your efforts to take these steps, remember that a proactive approach is better than a passive one. However, finding the motivation will not be easy, especially because you might be struggling with doubts and sadness, but the spiritual payoff will prove indispensable to your recovery.

Like a Death

Because the divorce process saturates people with toxic emotions like frustration, anger, resentment, guilt, shame, and lots of free-flowing anxiety and symptoms of depression, many divorced persons compare divorce to an unexpected death. Despite the strong stance on the eternal nature of marriage, the Church acknowledges that some marriages cease to be viable places in which those involved can "work out [their] salvation in fear and trembling" (Philippians 2:12). This comparison to death is especially true of the partner who did not initiate the divorce process and did not want it, although the initiating partner often experiences the same types of visceral reactions and feelings.

For the spouse who did not initiate the divorce process, the pending divorce is especially difficult to accept. One spouse I counseled put it this way: "Some days I feel so lost. My emotions range from anger to depression. I'm short with the kids, and I don't want to get up in the morning. It's terrible. It's sort of like someone died, but he didn't die. . . . I'm going to a funeral every time I meet with my attorney." Because divorce is like a death, a healthy, holy grieving process is often associated with divorce recovery.

The Grieving Process

Like the death of a loved one, the recovery process from divorce will require you to get in touch with your ambivalent feelings and grieve the loss. Many people have difficulty with this step. One woman I counseled vigorously objected when I suggested she take time to unpack her repressed emotions and lament her sins. "How do I do this? The kids need me. I have to get up and go to work

> LIKE THE DEATH OF A LOVED ONE, THE RECOVERY PROCESS FROM DIVORCE WILL REQUIRE YOU TO GET IN TOUCH WITH YOUR AMBIVALENT FEELINGS AND GRIEVE THE LOSS.

every day. . . . I feel like I need to attend to their needs right now and my needs have to come second." Another man said, "It's been almost a year since the divorce, and I haven't shed a tear. All I really have felt is numbness. I guess that's not too healthy. I want to cry, but the tears just won't come." In these instances, both needed to grieve their loss, and, with additional counseling, both eventually did grieve and felt the grieving process' cathartic, restorative effects. If you are like these two people and you have not grieved the loss of your marriage, I would suggest you find a way to do so.

The grieving process is different for each person. In some cases, it will be short in duration, and in other cases it will take more time. Whether the process is short or long, it cannot be rushed. So, give yourself permission to grieve through the entire process. An occasional release of some emotion is simply not enough.

> ON AVERAGE, RESEARCHERS SUGGEST THAT IT TAKES PEOPLE FIVE YEARS TO RECOVER FROM THE EMOTIONAL IMPACT OF A DIVORCE.

On average, researchers suggest that it takes people five years to recover from the emotional impact of a divorce (Everette & Lee 2006). One e-mail respondent stated, "The civil divorce took about a year. It's been three years since I received my divorce and I'm still fighting with my emotions. Without warning, some days I still feel some anger, and on other days I'm in the dumps."

Elizabeth Kubler Ross (1969), a pioneer in the hospice movement, identified the following stages of grieving and recovery. I have often used them in conjunction with the work I do with people who are struggling through the emotional side of divorce. They have proven helpful to these people, and they should prove helpful to you. In most cases, people do not seamlessly pass from one stage to another. Sometimes they are caught between one or more of the following steps simultaneously:

- **Denial.** When the "d" word (divorce) is broached, the first spouse (Spouse A) has a very hard time accepting it. Spouse A believes that his or her partner (Spouse B) will have a change of heart. In some instances this happens, but in most cases, once Spouse B has decided to divorce, his or her resolve is firm.

- **Anger/Resentment.** Once Spouse A understands that Spouse B does not intend to return and work on the marriage, Spouse A experiences high levels of anger and resentment. The anger and resentment are extremely toxic and pervasive, often affecting the interactions and transactions with Spouse B and others.

- **Bargaining.** In the midst of the anger and resentment, it is not unusual for Spouse A to try to bargain with Spouse B. In these instances, Spouse A might make promises and try to strike bargains to dissuade Spouse B from leaving. In most cases, these efforts fail.

- **Depression.** When a person realizes that there is nothing he or she can do to prevent the divorce, this person will generally experience symptoms of depression. In these instances, many people benefit from a physical, some medication, and some psychotherapy and spiritual counseling.

- **Acceptance.** After a lengthy period of struggle, which often requires cycling through many of these steps, most people will accept the inevitable and seek to piece their lives back together. It is at this point that many people begin to accept the emotional aspect of the divorce.

The Stigma of Divorce

Despite the high divorce rate and the fact that in our society divorce is viewed as an acceptable way of exiting a dysfunctional marriage, some divorced persons still attest to experiencing varying amounts of social stigma. This is especially true for people in high-profile positions, some religious people, and persons influenced by subcultures that condemn divorce.

The reality and pain of the stigma still attached to divorce is revealed in the following excerpt from an e-mail written by a Greek-American woman: "It's been almost two years. At first I didn't know how to face my family and church family. It was very awkward. I felt people were judging me; I also felt embarrassed and like a failure. People didn't really know what to say to me, and I had a hard time explaining what happened. Before the divorce, we were role models in our community. That changed during the separation and especially after the divorce. It was very awkward. But thankfully, as time passed, things got better and people were more understanding, but from time to time, I still feel some twinges of embarrassment and awkwardness when I meet people I haven't seen since the divorce." As this woman's observations suggest, social stigma is still alive and well in many sectors of our society, and divorced persons still encounter judgmental attitudes during their efforts to recover. Often, Greek Orthodox church communities are no exception.

As people recover from the effects of divorce, they are better able to handle the social stigma. After considerable work with a man whose second marriage ended in divorce, he stated the following with some pride: "Since my first wife died from cancer, when people asked if I was married, I would tell them I was a widower and didn't allude to my second marriage, which ended in divorce. I no longer do that. I simply tell them that my wife left me and I'm divorced. . . . Don't misunderstand me. I'm still concerned with what people think about me, but not nearly as much. So, if people ask, I just tell them that I'm divorced." It takes time to get to get to this place. If you are not there, do not become discouraged. As you intentionally expend the time and energy to recover from divorce, like this man, you will be able to cope with the stigma associated with divorce.

Post-divorce Examination

People who do not take the time to prayerfully process a divorce are generally destined to relive their mistakes if they remarry (Burns and Whiteman 1998). These people generally end up on the same slippery slope that led them toward their first marital meltdown and divorce. Taking the time to evaluate what went wrong and how you contributed to the divorce is time well spent.

One e-mail respondent shared the following with me after a lengthy e-mail exchange during her recovery: "I'm so glad I took the time to look at my sins after the divorce. Mind you now, it wasn't easy. For the first six to nine months after the divorce, I was fixated on him and what he did to me. Then my therapist came along and challenged me to look at my sins. At first, I resented this, but in time I realized it was sound counsel. I still remember the verse you quoted from Scripture when I asked you for a second opinion: 'First take the log out of your eye, and then you will see clearly to take the sliver out of your neighbor's eye' (Matthew 7:5). I took my therapist's advice and your second opinion to heart and began looking at my mistakes. . . . Swallowing humble pie and looking at my mistakes wasn't easy, but I won't be as likely to make them again if I remarry."

A handful of sessions—perhaps six to eight—with your pastor or a couples therapist should be sufficient to help you broaden your perspective on the events that led to the divorce, prayerfully process some very toxic feelings that can inhibit the recovery process after a divorce, and mitigate fears related to remarriage and another divorce.

The Children

Almost all parents who are casualties of divorce have heard that they should insulate their children from their conflicts. Unfortunately, research suggests that in a significant percentage of cases, parents end up demonizing the other parent (Marquardt 2005).

Some triangulate their children, placing them directly in the middle of their arguments, thus often forcing them to take sides. Often parents who are casualties of divorce engage in these and other similar unhealthy tactics because they are angry at one another and fearful that their relationship with their children will be irreparably compromised. So, if you are tempted to engage in any of these unproductive strategies, for your children's sake, avoid these temptations. These and other similar destructive traps will ultimately end up making you feel worse about yourself and will harm your children. The following guidelines should prove useful in your efforts to help your children during and after the divorce process:

> TO THE BEST OF YOUR ABILITY, KEEP CHILDREN AS WELL INSULATED AS POSSIBLE FROM THE EMOTIONAL FALLOUT THAT OCCURS BETWEEN THE TWO OF YOU DURING AND AFTER THE DIVORCE.

- Avoid the temptation to use the children as a bargaining chip to obtain leverage during and after the divorce. This is not conducive to children's best interests.

- To the best of your ability, keep children as well insulated as possible from the emotional fallout that occurs between the two of you during and after the divorce.

- Despite your best efforts to insulate your children, you cannot insulate them from all the fallout that accompanies divorce. Like you, your children will struggle with the painful process of divorce. Engaging in regular damage control is the best course of action to help them work through the negative residual effects.

- In your efforts to deal with the fallout, be prepared to answer your children's questions in an age-appropriate manner, and make certain they know they can come to you with their issues and problems. If they do not come to you, do not assume they are not suffering; they are. Go to them.

- Repeatedly assure your children that they are not responsible for the divorce. Many children silently suffer with the belief that they have caused the break-up of their parents' marriage.

- Reassure your children that God and you will always love them and be there for them. This consistent, unending, dependable stream of love "bears all things, hopes all things, endures all things" (1 Corinthians 13:7).

- Despite your best efforts, your child may need additional assistance while working through the emotional fallout associated with the divorce. Profes-sional counselors who are trained to work with children and their families can make a difference. When seeking professional help, always consider a thera-pist's training and experience. Ask a few simple questions, like: "How much of your caseload involves children and their families?" "How much experience do you have working with children whose parents have divorced?" "Are you comfortable working with religious populations?" If the therapist's answers do not satisfy you, continue your search. Marriage and family therapists, social workers, clinical psychologists, and professional counselors who do play therapy and also work with parents are well equipped to help.

After struggling for years through a very contentious divorce process, one mother's remarks illustrate how parents can compound the pain and suffering that accompanies the divorce process. "He's turned my two girls against me and convinced them that I am an evil, loose woman. My oldest has been especially brainwashed. He's used the Bible like a sledgehammer to break up any meaningful connection between us. After obtaining counsel from a very conservative religious group, my daughter's father has convinced my two girls that divorce is wrong and that I am living in sin because I remarried. They don't care that he was physically abusive and highly manipulative. They don't care that I worked to put the food on the table for years and he stayed home doing nothing. They just think that I'm a sinner—even after I got a church divorce. It's been a real nightmare. I haven't had contact with them in months. . . . The worst is that I believe these kids—now twelve and fifteen—will grow up really, really damaged."

There are many books written from a child's point of view that chronicle the pain and suffering that children experience. One resource I often recommend is Elizabeth Marquardt's book entitled *Between Two Worlds: The Inner Lives of Children of Divorce.*

Life after Divorce

In order to regain perspective and some emotional, psychological, and spiritual stability, you must walk through a process, painful as it may be (Burns and Whiteman 1998; Splinter 1992). I have asked a number of people who passed through the divorce process to respond to the question "Is there life after divorce?" Here are some of their comments:

> *"I never thought the pain would end. Slowly, as I did my part and confessed my sins and sought a better life, I was able to dig myself out of the pain and suffering. If you're going through a divorce, hang in there. It gets better."*

> *"I never thought I could show my face at church again. It was amazing how much support I got when I did. Not from everyone, mind you, but from a select few. I never expected comfort and support from some of the people who approached me. It was great. It helped a lot."*

"The old adage 'Time heals all wounds' applies here. Tell them it will take time and some considerable effort. If you do your part, it gets better."

"In time you gain perspective and see things as they were rather than in a skewed perspective. In the beginning I thought it was all her fault. In time, you'll see that you did some things, and she did some things that killed the marriage. Once you get past some of that and gain a better perspective, your view of the future begins to change—it gets better."

"Is there life after divorce? Absolutely! Sooner or later you stop feeling sorry for yourself and you stop wondering about what could have been, and you start looking at life after divorce. That's when life gets exciting."

Getting Back into Good Standing with the Church

As you may or may not know, when Greek Orthodox Christians divorce, they lose their good standing in the Church and must obtain an ecclesiastical divorce in order to regain it. As stated in the *2012 Yearbook* published by the Greek Orthodox Archdiocese of America, "Orthodox Christians who have obtained a civil divorce but not an ecclesiastical divorce may not participate in any sacraments or serve on the Parish Council, Archdiocesan District Council, Metropolis Council or Archdiocesan Council until they have been granted a divorce by the Church" (Costidis 2012, 268). (By the way, this process varies from one Orthodox jurisdiction to the next. Please check with your priest if you are not

> AN ECCLESIASTICAL DIVORCE . . . PERMITS ORTHODOX CHRISTIANS THE OPPORTUNITY TO REGAIN GOOD STANDING IN THE CHURCH AND TO RESTORE THEIR RELATIONSHIP WITH GOD.

part of the Greek Orthodox Archdiocese of America. He will be in the best position to outline what is required of you after you obtain a civil divorce.)

The process of obtaining an ecclesiastical divorce is not complicated. However, when Greek Orthodox Christians find out that this additional step must also be negotiated, many are not interested in revisiting the painful circumstances surrounding their divorce. Some even resent this requirement. Here are some typical reactions:

"I have to do what? That's not fair. I don't want to go back and rehash everything with my priest. It will be painfully embarrassing."

"I won't do it—plain and simple. I would think that the Church would be more understanding and not require this."

"I don't want to air my dirty laundry in front of my priest. I'm afraid the priest will tell others what happened."

"Alright, but I'm not happy about the fact that a tax is attached to this process!"

Despite these and other visceral reactions that some Greek Orthodox have about obtaining an ecclesiastical divorce, the Church has sound reasons for requiring its faithful to take this step. First, it affords its faithful the opportunity to prayerfully put closure on a painful chapter in their lives. Up to this point, divorced persons have found closure legally, emotionally, and psychologically. However, many fail to obtain closure spiritually and ecclesiastically. This step permits Orthodox Christians the opportunity to regain good standing in the Church and to restore their relationship with God. All too often, many neglect to consider the value of repenting and receiving God's forgiveness. These steps are as important as any others in the recovery process after a divorce.

Conclusion

The statement "We are all a work in progress" is a fitting end to this chapter. No matter where you are in the divorce process, remember that everyone is a work in progress. Our loving God does not wish that we remain mired in the destructive emotional, psychological, and spiritual fallout associated with divorce. That is ultimately why,

> "WE ARE ALL A WORK IN PROGRESS."

in the words of some fathers of our Church, He took on flesh and became like us that we might become like Him. Yes, we are all sinners, and we all make mistakes that we regret, but we are also God's children. So the Church, in the spirit of God's restorative message, understands that we deserve a second chance.

What has happened cannot be changed. However, while you struggle to recover from divorce, learn from your mistakes, ask God for mercy and forgiveness, and embrace the undying, unconditional love He has for you: to God's glory and our salvation. Amen.

Questions for Reflection

- How do you reconcile the Church's stance on divorce with the reality of divorce?

- How do you understand divorce to be like a death?

- What do you think about the steps toward recovery from divorce?

- Where are God and the Church in your life as you seek to recover from divorce?

- If children are involved, how can you attend to each of their needs and your own needs while going through a divorce?

- How can your pastor support you through the process of a divorce?

RECOMMENDED READING

- **The Fresh Start: Divorce Recovery Workbook.** Burns, B., and T. Whiteman. 1998. Nashville: Thomas Nelson Publishers.

- **2012 Yearbook: Greek Orthodox Archdiocese of America.** Costidis, M., ed. 2012. New York: Greek Orthodox Archdiocese of America.

- **When Marriages Fail: Systemic Family Therapy Interventions and Issues; A Tribute to William C. Nicholas.** Everett, C. A., and R. E. Lee. 2006. New York: Haworth Press.

- **The State of Our Unions 2006: The Social Health of Marriage in America.** Dafoe Whitehead, B., and D. Popenoe. 2006. Retrieved July 14, 2006. http://marriage.rutgers.edu/Publications/Priont/PrintSOOU2006.htm.

- **What Predicts Divorce?** Gottman, J. M. 1994. Hillsdale, NJ: Erlbaum.

- **On Death and Dying.** Kubler Ross, E. 1969. New York: Touchstone.

- **Between Two Worlds: The Inner Lives of Children of Divorce.** Marquardt, E. 2005. New York: Crown Publishers.

USEFUL WEBSITES

www.divorcecare.com

www.smartmarriages.com

REMARRIAGE AND STEPFAMILY CHALLENGES

"For everything there is a season, and a time
for every matter under heaven." –Ecclesiastes 3:1

Joe and Katherine

Joe (42) and Katherine (47) have arrived at their first therapy session. As the therapist assesses their situation, the following information emerges.

Joe and Katherine have been married for three months and are considering separation and divorce. Before getting married, they dated for one month. This is Joe's second marriage. Joe states, "My first marriage ended badly. She's still in my life making me miserable." Katherine was involved in one long-term live-in relationship prior to meeting Joe, but she has never been married. Her partner recently died after a long struggle with cancer. As she fondly remembers him, she states, "It was devastating to lose him. In many ways, he can never be re-placed. We were true soul mates."

Katherine has one son, Thomas (15). Joe has two teens, his son Mason (19) and his daughter Marissa (16). Mason lives with his mother; Thomas and Marissa live with the couple. Katherine expresses her uneasiness over the tension be-tween her son and Joe's children. She states, "Thomas and Marissa almost had a physical altercation the other day." Katherine detests violence and is concerned that the conflict could become violent. She adds, "It feels like it could turn ugly at any time." Joe does not see things in the same way. He maintains that "they'll eventually work things out." Katherine frowns and rolls her eyes at this remark.

To complicate matters, the couple lives in a modest rental owned by Joe's par-ents and located right behind their home. Katherine observes, "His parents don't respect our privacy and are always popping in unannounced. I just can't live this way." Joe minimizes her complaint, saying, "It's no big deal. Hey, they're my parents! What do you want me to do, tell them to stay away?" Katherine rolls her eyes again and appears agitated.

When asked how they believe therapy might help, they both say, "We argue a lot and can't communicate." Then Joe states, "Finances are tight for me because I'm currently unemployed. Katherine continues to work, but we don't have a joint bank account." Katherine adds, "In addition to our communication problems,

I'd like to work on issues related to parenting and Joe's parents' constant intrusions." Additionally, Joe would like "more sex," and Katherine desires "more intimacy and understanding."

As the assessment continues, the therapist identifies the following individual and couple strengths. Joe seems quite personable and is somewhat laid back—perhaps too laid back. He values hard work and has recently "accepted Jesus." He states, "These days, I pray a lot and read Holy Scripture. Besides Katherine, it's what I have to hang onto." Katherine is a lapsed Greek Orthodox Christian who considers herself "spiritual, but not religious." She is intelligent and quite articulate. She considers herself a patient person who "lives and lets live." Nevertheless, she says, "These last few months have taxed my patience and shown me some things about myself that I don't like." Like Joe, she is invested in trying to save the marriage, but she is more dubious about their future together.

Joe and Katherine's therapy lasted ten sessions. During the last few sessions, they realized that their differences were much too large to overcome and they could not make the needed adjustments. They also wondered if they would have either slowed down their relationship or not married had they taken the time to consider the promises and pitfalls of remarriage and stepfamily life. Despite their affection for each other prior to marriage, their mutual love was profoundly challenged and undermined by the many remarriage and stepfamily issues and problems that quickly emerged after marriage—issues and problems that proved to be intractable and insurmountable. As a result, six months after this couple married, Katherine filed for divorce.

The Complexities of Remarriage and Stepfamily Life

As Joe and Katherine's story suggests, remarried couples with children from previous relationships encounter a host of unique and complex challenges. Given these realities, if you are contemplating remarriage, keep in mind the following question as you read the remainder of this chapter: How does this information relate to us/me? Careful, prayerful, intentional decisions, along with the love you share with the person you are thinking about marrying, can make all the difference in determining whether you succeed or fail as a couple and stepfamily. The bottom line is, as with Joe and Katherine, many remarried spouses and couples fail to make careful and inten-

> REMARRIED COUPLES WITH CHILDREN FROM PREVIOUS RELATIONSHIPS ENCOUNTER A HOST OF UNIQUE AND COMPLEX CHALLENGES.

tional decisions and become victims of the old adage "What love conceals, time will reveal."

In addition, after reviewing the information that follows, consider the possibility of premarital preparation and education. An educational resource entitled *The Journey of Marriage in the Orthodox Church*, written by Dr. Philip Mamalakis and Rev. Dr. Charles Joanides, may be helpful. For some, this workbook will not be sufficient to address all concerns and needs. If not, it would behoove you to find a couples therapist who has been trained to administer PREPARE/ENRICH or FOCUS. These instruments are more sophisticated, and, together with *The Journey of Marriage,* can provide a more comprehensive, Christ-centered, and evidence-based assessment of your current strengths and weaknesses, along with feedback sessions to build on your strengths and to address areas where growth is needed.

Factors That Cause Second Marriages and Stepfamilies to Fail

Limited Time to Adjust to Married Life

After the honeymoon is over, remarried couples literally hit the ground running. Suddenly, the needs of children from previous marriages and a host of step-family challenges take precedence over the marriage. These unique needs and challenges rob remarried couples of the time required to adjust to married life and cultivate oneness. Unless couples make a concerted effort to find time for one another, marital satisfaction suffers, and, by extension, the stepfamilies also suffer.

A Polarizing Effect

The structure of stepfamilies creates intense, highly polarized insider and out-sider positions that make it much more difficult for these families to coalesce and form a new, stable family unit. For example, let's suppose that a newly remarried couple that includes a husband who is Greek Orthodox and a wife who is nominally Episcopalian—as well as her two children, both baptized in the Mormon Church—decides to worship in the Greek Orthodox Church. Due to religious differences, this family will be faced with a host of challenges that can seriously compromise religious and spiritual development and undermine family unity. Some typical challenges this family might encounter include: (1) The children's biological father might adamantly object to his children worshipping in the Greek Orthodox Church. (2) The children might feel as though they are betraying their father when attending the Greek Orthodox Church. (3) The children's discomfort could prompt their mother to discontinue family worship in the Greek Orthodox Church. (4) The Greek Orthodox husband might interpret the biological father's reaction as intrusive and insulting. (5) The Greek Orthodox father might feel betrayed and resent his wife for acquiescing to her ex-spouse's complaints.

Children's Losses and Loyalty Bonds

Children encounter losses and conflicted loyalty bonds when stepfamilies form. It is not uncommon for children—especially older children—to have mixed feelings when trying to form an intimate relationship with their biological parent's new spouse. In fact, children often report feeling as though they are betraying their biological mother or father when they become closer to their parent's new spouse. This dynamic creates a lingering emotional distance between stepfamily members that is not easily bridged.

Different Parenting Styles

Differences in parenting styles create a lingering, often unresolved tension between remarried couples that undermines both marital satisfaction and the efforts of couples to parent the children in a consistent, effective, and supportive manner. With regard to this challenge, the best outcome occurs when couples manage to find some common ground they can agree upon to help them parent the children. This common ground is usually established after remarried couples have expended considerable time and effort seeking compromise. Conversely, the worst outcome occurs when couples cannot find any middle ground. In these cases, protracted couple conflict lingers.

Shared Family Values

Stepfamilies encounter challenges in their efforts to establish shared family values and culture. A stepfamily that is comprised of some children who have been baptized and raised in a Greek Orthodox church and others who have been raised in a Jewish home, for example, will likely encounter numerous unique challenges as they try to cultivate religious, cultural, and family traditions that fit well with all family members.

Family Boundaries

Family boundaries tend to be different in stepfamilies when compared to first-time married couples and their nuclear families. Boundaries in stepfamilies will often extend to include one or more other parents who affect everything from vacation planning, to whether children have their homework assignments completed, to decisions about children attending church camp.

How Can the Church Help?

Despite all the challenges facing remarried couples and stepfamilies, especially those that involve differences in religious beliefs and practices, the Church can support and help remarried spouses, couples, and their stepfamilies both before and after they form. Below you will find some suggested ways in which the Church can be of assistance.

An Orthodox Perspective on Marriage

Clergy have a Christ-centered perspective on marriage that can serve to profoundly broaden and strengthen engaged and remarried couples' perspectives on marriage. For example, when divorced persons who desire to remarry become intimately aware of Christ-like love, patience, kindness, and forgiveness, these and other God-given, timeless fruits of God's Holy Spirit can prove indispensable to remarried couples in their efforts to cultivate marital oneness and family well-being.

Owning Our Past Mistakes

Much of the existing literature related to remarriage indicates that many divorced persons fail to carefully examine the factors that caused their first marriage to end. As a result, many divorced persons end up reliving past mistakes when they remarry. In an effort to avoid this, divorced persons might consider consulting their priest to help them identify how their past mistakes contributed to the slippery slope toward marital meltdown and divorce. By guiding them to increased insight, forgiveness, and repentance, their priest can help divorced persons to be liberated from any residual guilt and shame they harbor related to the sins and mistakes they made in a former marriage.

Collaboration with Professionals

If clergy are not personally equipped to help counsel and educate persons desiring remarriage, at minimum they may be able either to collaborate with trusted professionals in their local community who have this expertise or to simply choose to refer divorced persons to professionals who specialize in helping individuals and couples acquire a broader understanding of the inherent challenges they will encounter when they remarry. In either case, prior to remarriage, counseling can prove infinitely helpful to individuals, couples, children, and adolescents in their efforts to adjust to stepfamily life.

Conclusion

Obviously, the best remedy for dealing with remarriage and stepfamily issues is for first-time married people to attend to the needs of their spouse and their marriage daily. However, when marriages fail, the second-best approach is for divorced persons to prayerfully consider the many pitfalls and promises of remarriage and stepfamily life prior to remarrying. A prayerful, faithful approach can prove indispensable in their efforts to protect and promote marital oneness and stepfamily unity and well-being.

Questions for Reflection

• If you are considering remarriage and children are involved, what steps have you taken to prepare for the marriage and the unique challenges it will bring for you, your future spouse, and the children?

• If you are remarried with children involved, which unique challenges resonate with you, and what are you doing to address them?

• Given your situation, how can the Church support you and your family?

RECOMMENDED READING

• *Stepfamilies: Love, Marriage and Parenting in the First Decade.* Bray, J., and J. Kelly. 1999. New York: Broadway Books.

• *How to Talk so Kids Will Listen and Listen so Kids Will Talk.* Faber, A., and E. Mazlish. 1999. New York: Avon Books.

• *The Journey of Marriage in the Orthodox Church.* Mamalakis, P., and C. Joanides. 2011. New York: Greek Orthodox Archdiocese of America.

• *Mom's House, Dad's House: Making Two Homes for Your Child.* Ricci, I. 1997. New York: Simon & Schuster.

• *Custody Chaos, Personal Peace: Sharing Custody with Your Ex Who Is Driving You Crazy.* Wittman, J. P. 2001. New York: Penguin.

HELPFUL WEBSITES

www.smartmarriage.com
www.marriagefriendlytherapists.com
www.prepare-enrich.com
www.foccusinc.com